THE TEXTILE MANUFACTURERS OF INDIA

THE
TEXTILE MANUFACTURERS
OF
INDIA:

JOHN FORBES WATSON

18 VOLUMES
IN TWO BINDING
10 TO 18 VOLUMES

GYAN

Published by

Gyan Publishing House
5, Ansari Road
Daryaganj, New Delhi-110002
Phone: 011-47034999, 9811692060
E-mail: books@gyanbooks.com

Distribution Network
gyanbooks.com
India, USA, Canada, UK, Australia

ISBN: 978-93-7014-589-4 (Set) PB
978-93-7014-053-0 (10 to 18 Vols.) PB
First Published, 1866

2nd Impression 2025

Printed at: Gyan Press, Delhi.

THE TEXTILE MANUFACTURERS OF INDIA (10 to 18 Vols. in Two Binding)
Author: JOHN FORBES WATSON

THE TEXTILE MANUFACTURERS OF INDIA

JOHN FORBES WATSON

VOLUME:-10

1866

~~Prov. No. 356.~~ No. 361

INDIA FABRICS.

COTTON GOODS.

Kerchief worn on head and shoulders.

HALF DYE. EIGHT WOVEN IN A PIECE.

Single one 33 inches by 35 inches. Weight of one, 2½ oz. Price 8*d.* each.

From COONATOOR; MADRAS.

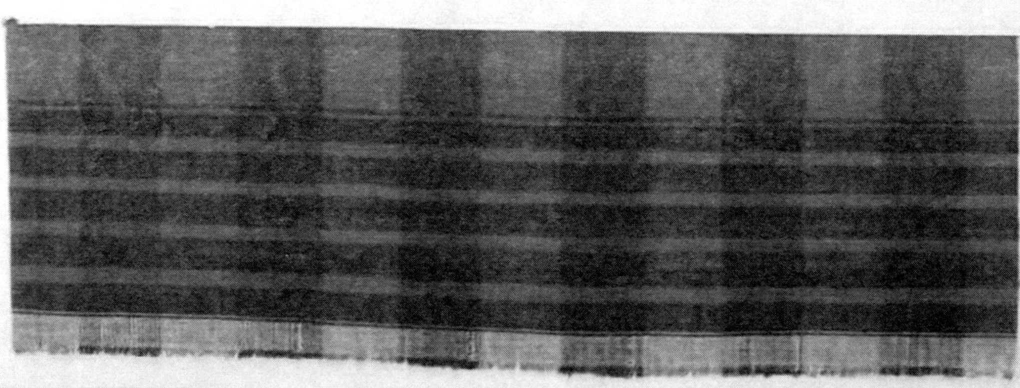

~~Prov. No. 168.~~ No. 362

INDIA FABRICS.

COTTON GOODS.

Kerchiefs for the head and shoulders. Fast colors.

EIGHT WOVEN IN A PIECE.

Length of each kerchief 30 inches ; width 28 inches. Weight of single one 3¾ oz. Price 7½d. each.

From COONATOOR; MADRAS.

~~Prov. No. 170.~~ No. 363

INDIA FABRICS.

COTTON GOODS.

Cotton neckkerchief to cover head and shoulders.

The glaze is obtained by means of a chank shell rubbed over the fabric. Eight woven in a piece.

Length or measure 1 yard square. Weight of single one 3 oz. Price $7\frac{1}{2}d$.

From VENTAPOLLUM ; MADRAS.

~~Prov. No. 171.~~ No. 364

INDIA FABRICS.

COTTON GOODS.

Cotton neckkerchiefs; glazed by means of a chank shell rubbed over it.

WORN OVER HEAD AND SHOULDERS. EIGHT WOVEN IN A PIECE.

Each one measures 1 yard square. Weight 3¾ oz. Price of single one 7½d.

From VENTAPOLLUM; MADRAS.

~~Prov. No. 172.~~ No. 355

INDIA FABRICS.

COTTON GOODS.

Cotton neckkerchief to cover head and shoulders.

Glaze obtained by chank shell rubbed over the fabric. Eight woven in a piece.

Single one measures 1 yard square. Weight of single one 3½ oz. Piece of each 7½*d*.

From VENTAPOLLUM; MADRAS.

~~Prov. No. 169.~~ No. 355

INDIA FABRICS.

COTTON GOODS.

Cotton neckkerchief worn over head and shoulders.

Glazed by means of a chank shell passed over the fabric. Eight woven in a piece.

Single one measures 1 yard square. Weight of single one 3½ oz. Price of each 1s. 1½d.

From VENTAPOLLUM; MADRAS.

~~Prov. No. 94.~~ No. 367

INDIA FABRICS.

CHINTZES.

Cotton printed glazed chintz, with an end for covering the head and shoulders.

WORN BY MALAY WOMEN.

Length 3 yards; width 1 yard. Weight 12 oz. Price 1s. 6d.

From ARCOT; MADRAS.

~~Prov. No. 392.~~ No. 368

INDIA FABRICS.

PIECE GOODS.

Cotton print.

Length 3 yards 24 inches; width 1 yard 5 inches. Weight $15\frac{3}{4}$ oz. Price 2s.

From MASULIPATAM; MADRAS.

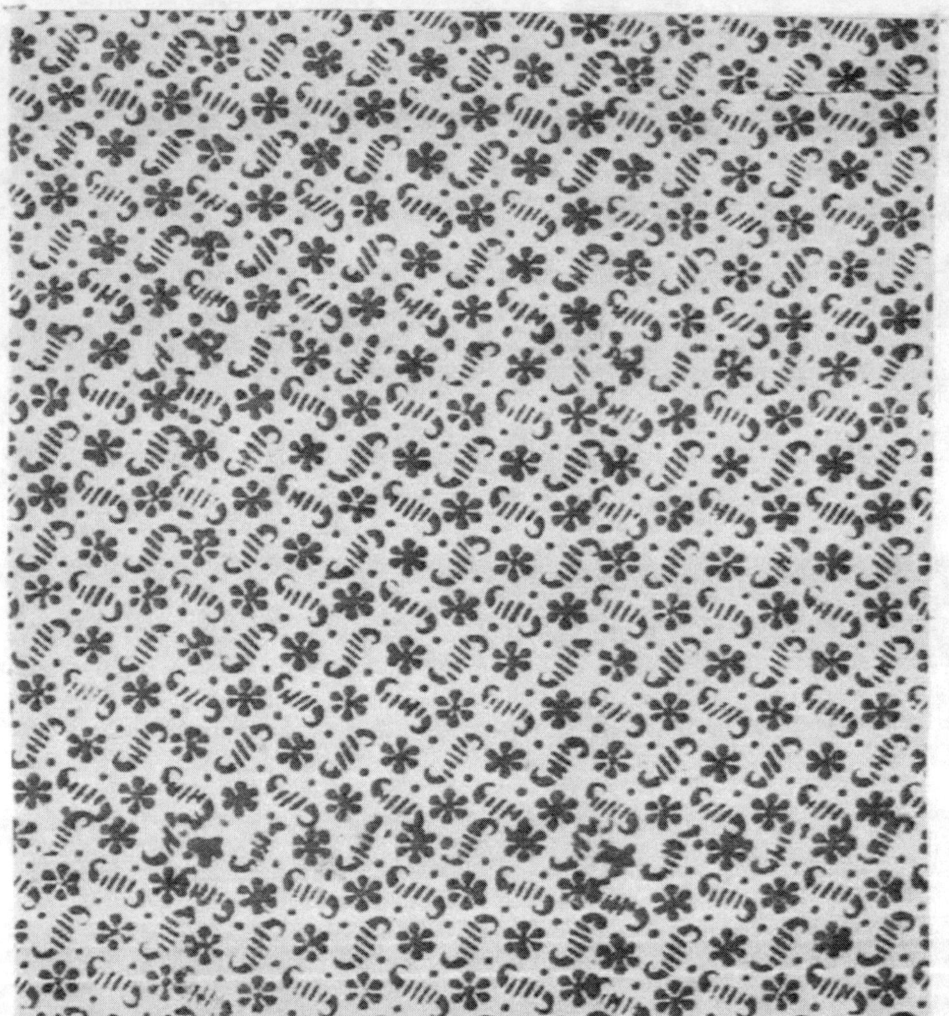

Prov. No. 333. No. 359

INDIA FABRICS.

PIECE GOODS.

Cotton print; coarse.

Length 5 yards 28 inches; width 1 yard 1 inch. Weight 1 lb. 5 oz. Price 3s. 9d.

From MASULIPATAM; MADRAS.

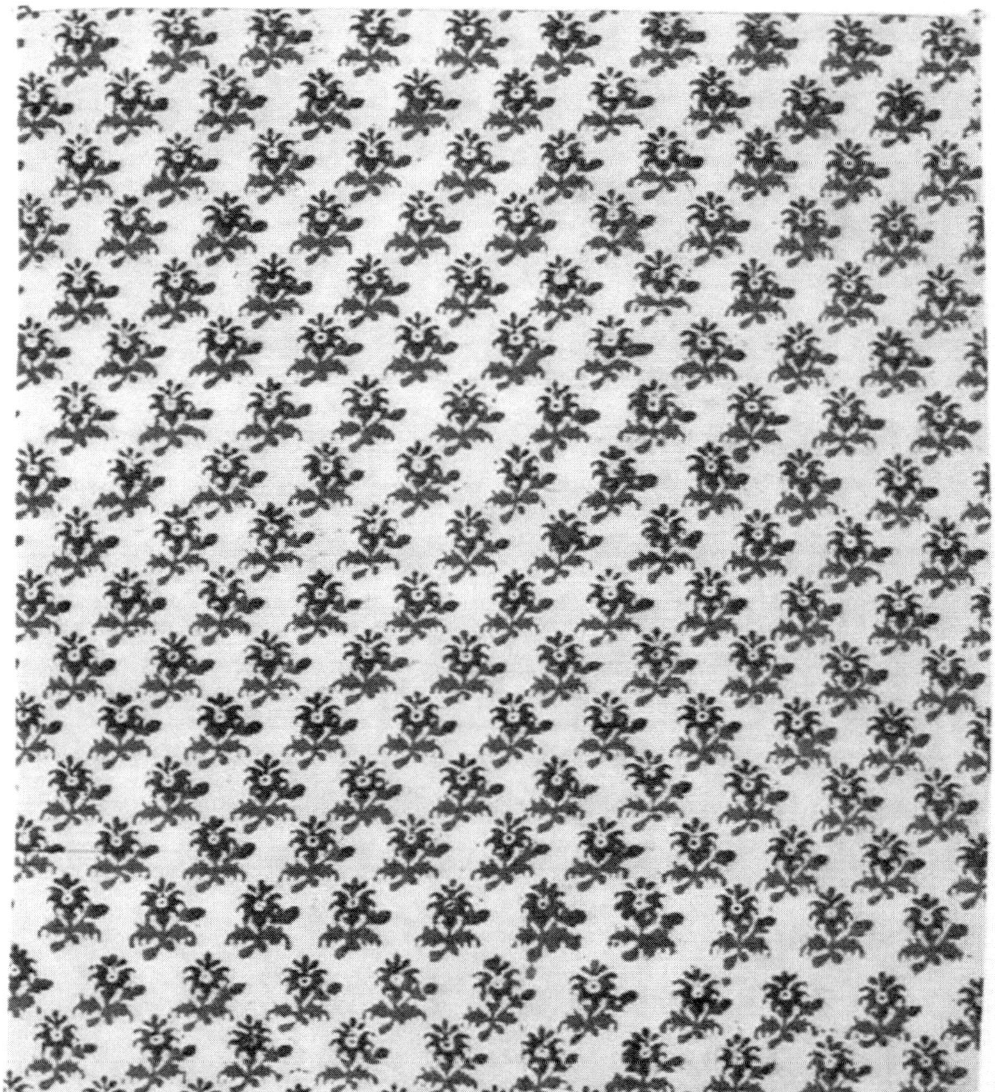

~~Prov. No. 132.~~ No. 370

INDIA FABRICS.

CHINTZES.

Cotton printed glazed chintz.

GOOD PATTERN AND MATERIAL.

Length 3 yards 27 inches; width 1 yard 2 inches. Price 8s.

From MASULIPATAM; MADRAS.

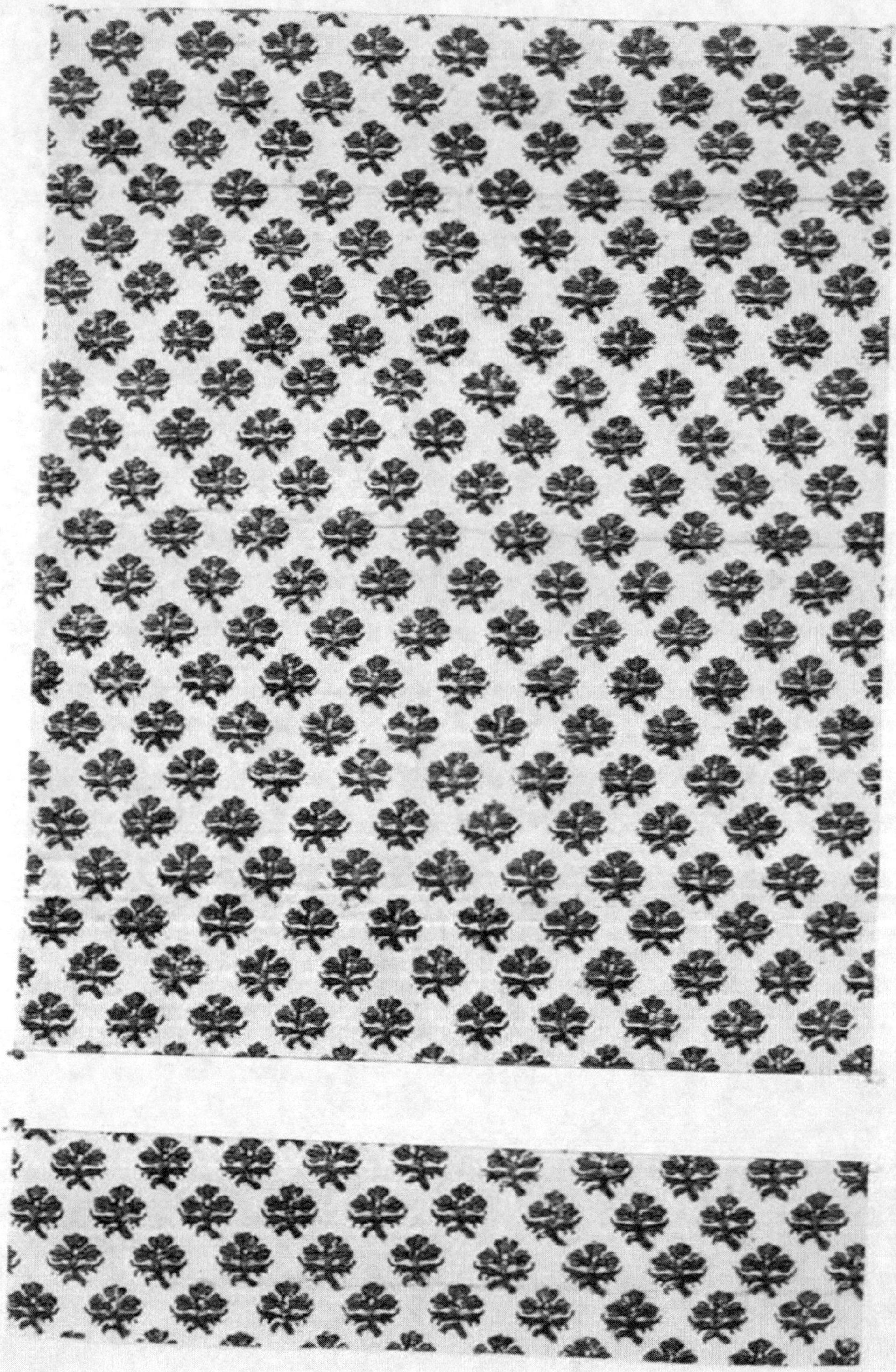

~~Prov. No. 93.~~ No. 371

INDIA FABRICS.

COTTON GOODS.

Cotton printed fabric, with end pattern.

Length 4 yards 18 inches ; width 1 yard. Weight 15 oz. Price 4s.

From MADRAS.

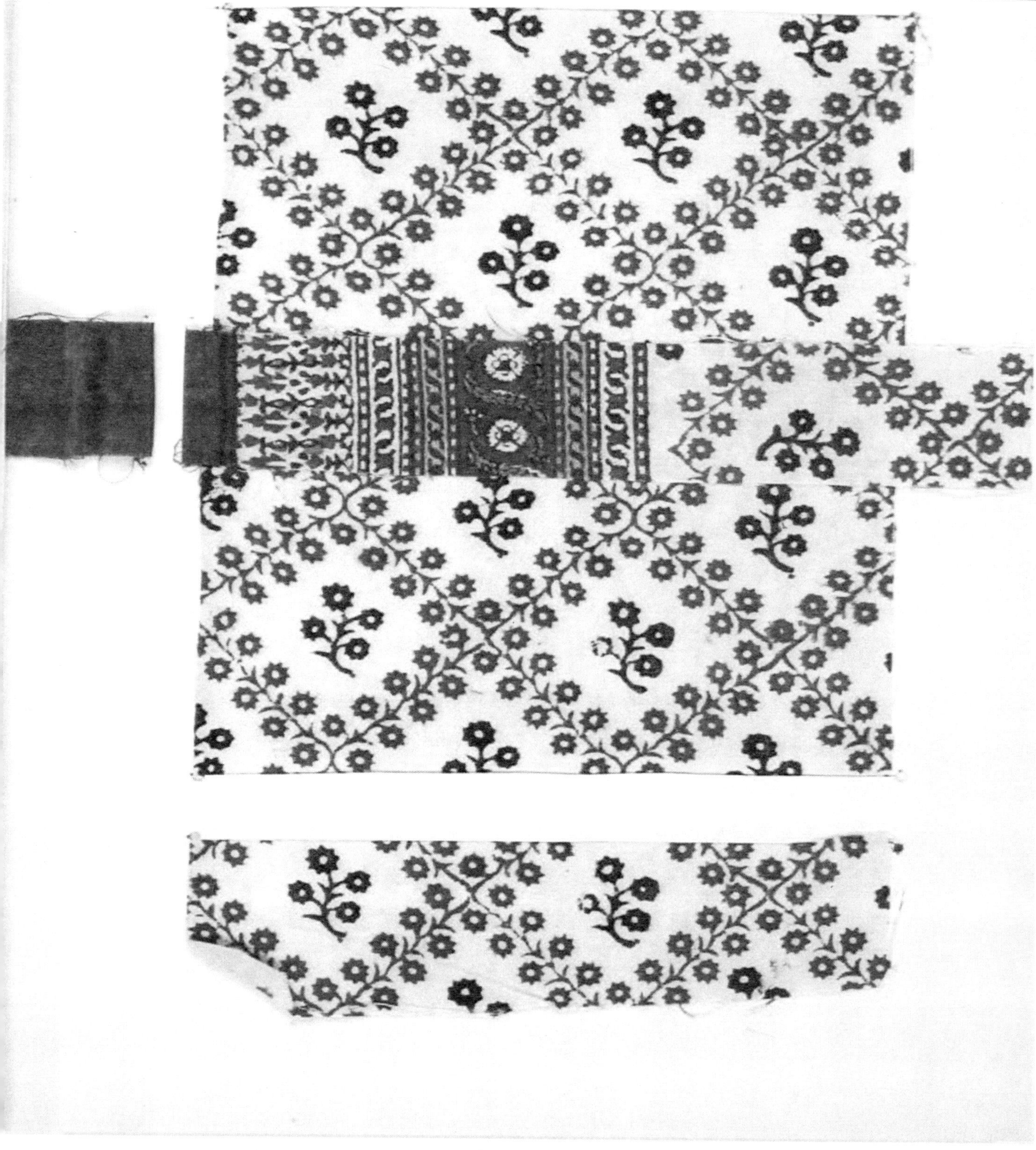

~~Prov. No. 158.~~ No. 372

INDIA FABRICS.

PIECE GOODS.

Cotton print. Used for petticoats.

Length 7 yards 18 inches; width 1 yard. Weight 1 lb. 12 oz. Price 3s. 1½d.

From BELLARY; MADRAS.

~~Prov. No. 66.~~ No. 373

INDIA FABRICS.

PIECE GOODS.

Cotton print; good pattern.

Length 4 yards; width 1 yard 6 inches. Weight 1 lb. 1 oz. Price 2s. 7½d.

From PONNARY; MADRAS.

~~Prov. No. 160.~~ No. 374

INDIA FABRICS.

PIECE GOODS.

Cotton print, coarse fabric, called "chetee" (chintz).

Length 7 yards; width 30 inches. Weight 1 lb. 7 oz. Price 2s.

From ARCOT; MADRAS.

Prov. No. 89. No. 375

INDIA FABRICS.

PIECE GOODS.

Cotton print (coarse), called "chetee" (chintz).

Length 9 yards; width 1 yard. Weight 2 lbs. 10 oz. Price 4s. 1½d.

From PONNARY; MADRAS.

~~Prov. No. 161.~~ No. 376

INDIA FABRICS.

PIECE GOODS.

Cotton print (coarse), called "chetee" (chintz).

Length 3 yards 18 inches; width 1 yard 6 inches. Weight 14 oz. Price 2s. 1½d.

From PONNARY; MADRAS.

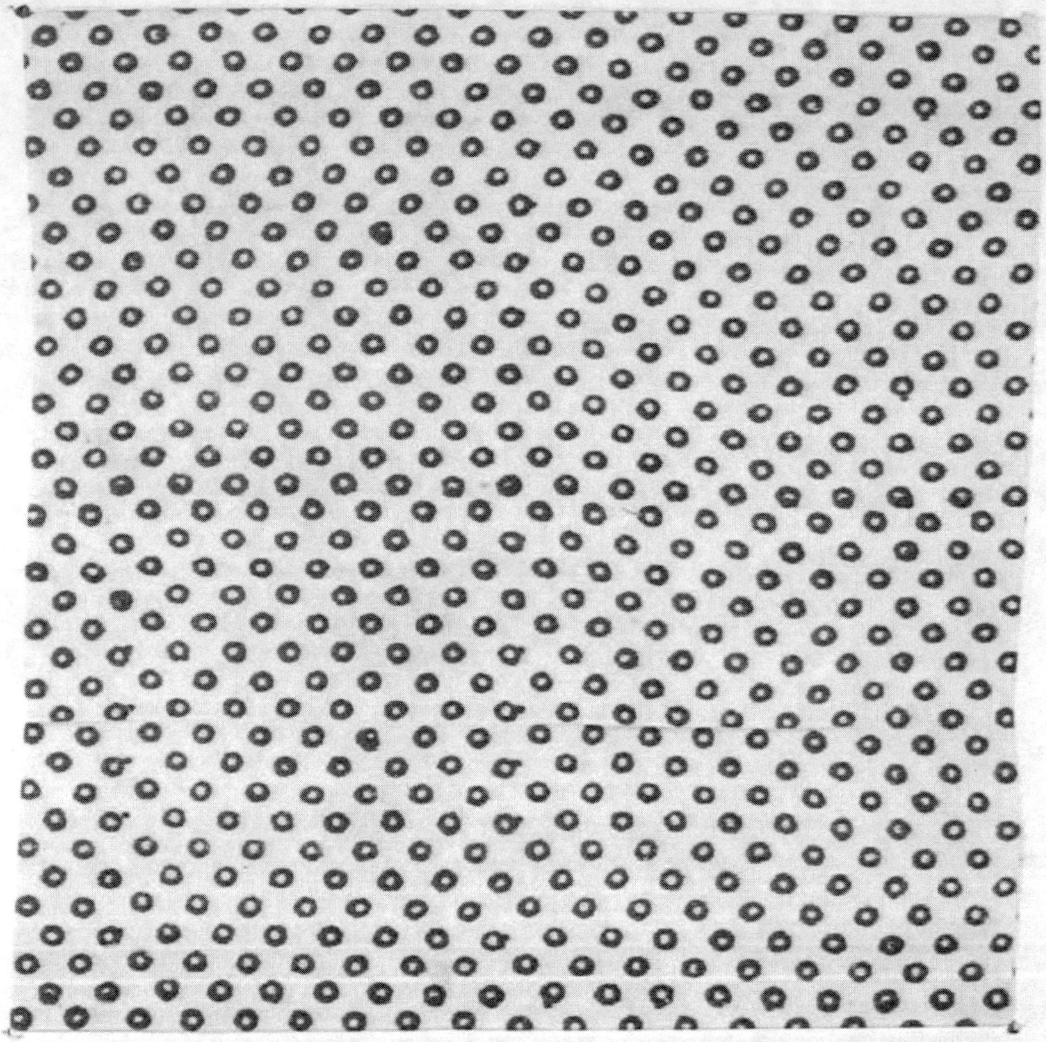

~~Paris No. 157.~~ No. 377

INDIA FABRICS.

PIECE GOODS.

Cotton print, called "chetee" (chintz).

Length 3 yards 18 inches; width 1 yard 8 inches. Weight 14 oz. Price 2s.

From ARCOT; MADRAS.

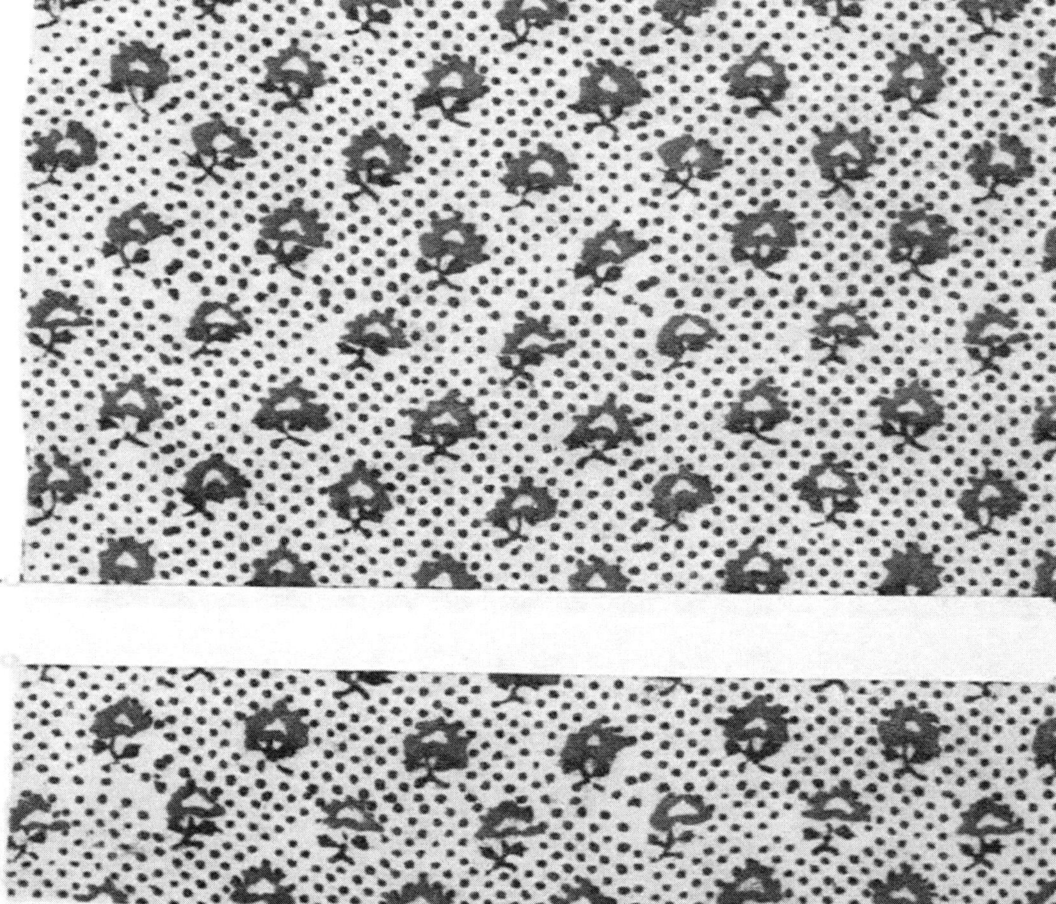

~~Prov. No. 156.~~ No. 378

INDIA FABRICS.

PIECE GOODS.

Cotton print, called "chetee" (chintz).

Length 3 yards 18 inches; width 1 yard 8 inches. Weight 14 oz. Price 2s.

From ARCOT; MADRAS.

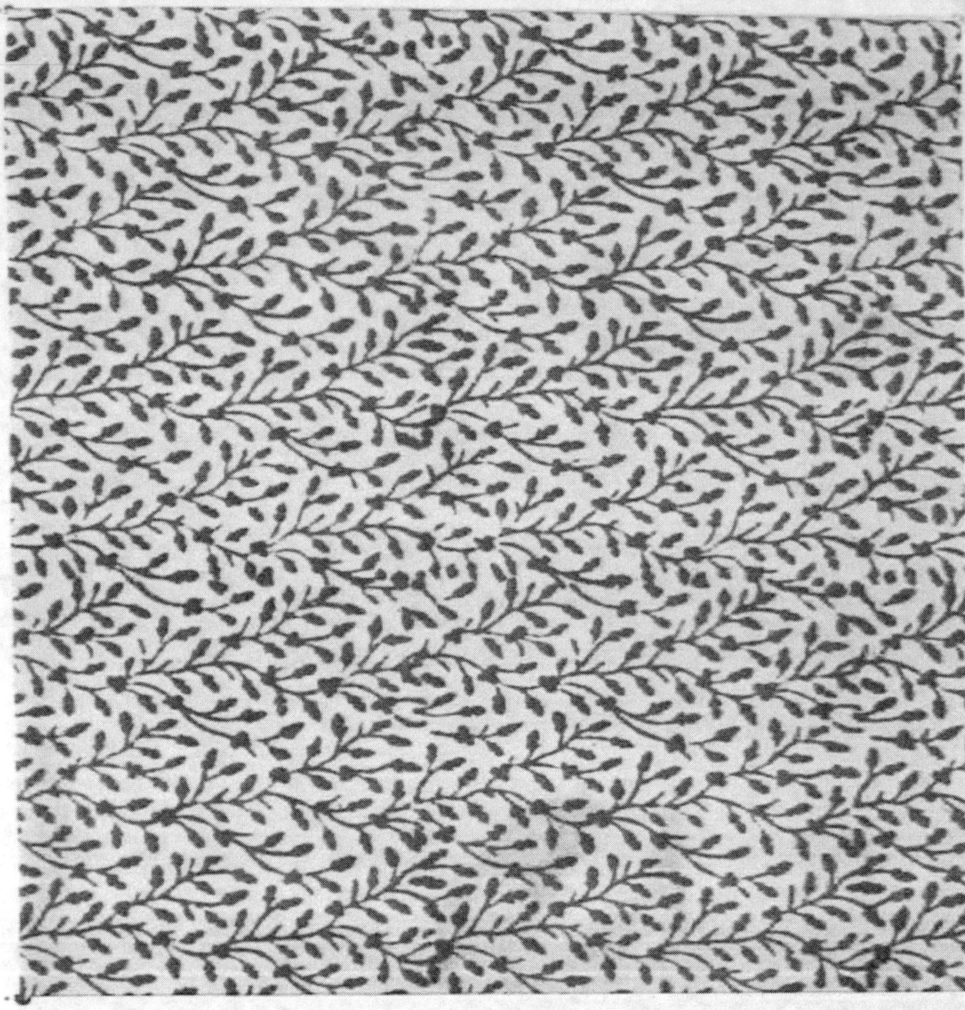

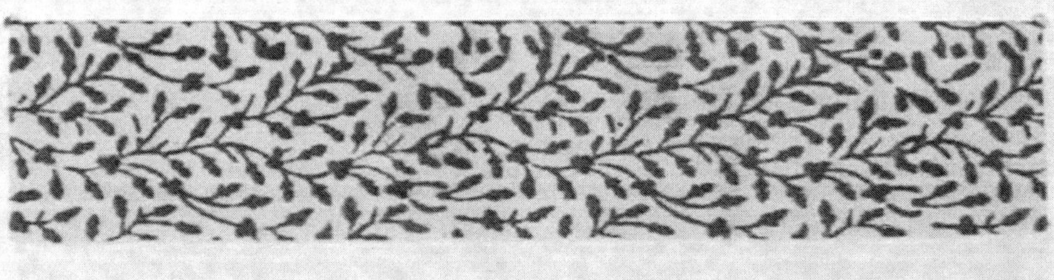

~~Prov. No. 163.~~ No. 379

INDIA FABRICS.

PIECE GOODS.

Cotton print (imperfectly).

Length 2 yards 18 inches; width 1 yard 2 inches. Weight 12 oz. Price 2s.

From ARCOT; MADRAS.

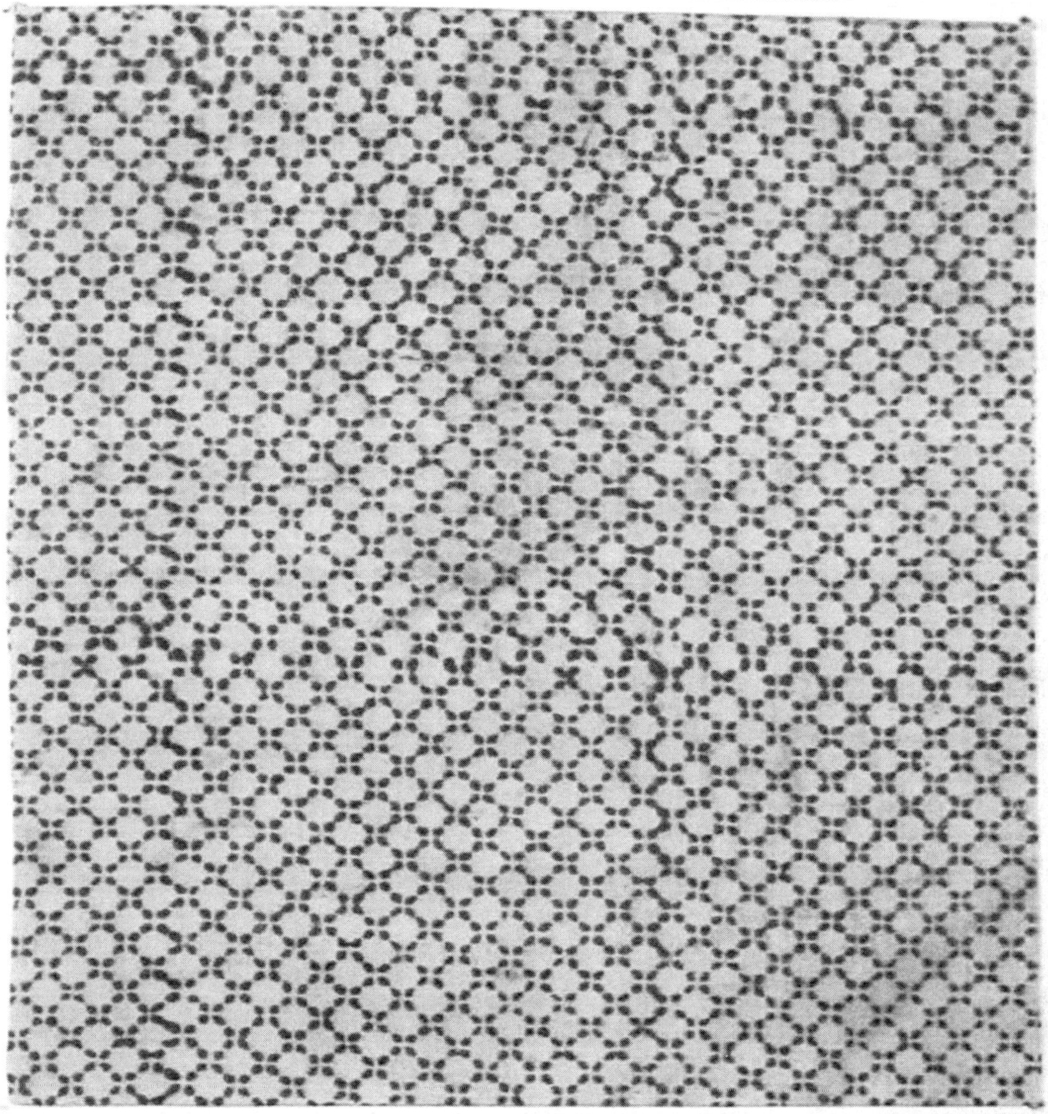

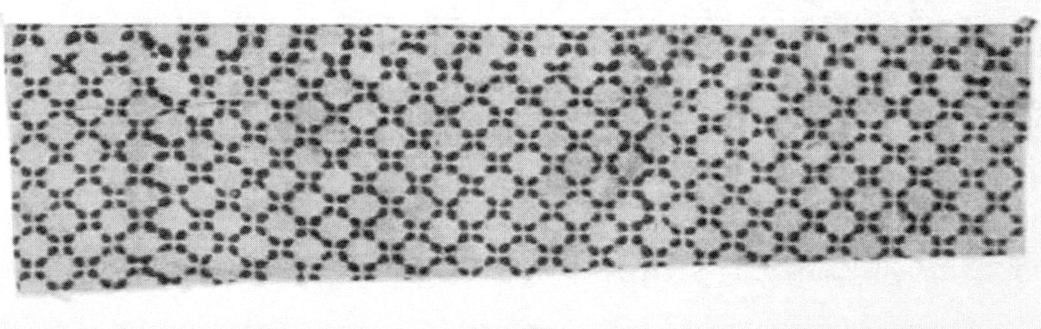

~~Prov. No. 154.~~ No. 380

INDIA FABRICS.

PIECE GOODS.

Cotton print.

Length 4 yards 18 inches; width 1 yard 4 inches. Weight 1 lb. 3 oz. Price 3s. 1½d.

From PONNARY; MADRAS.

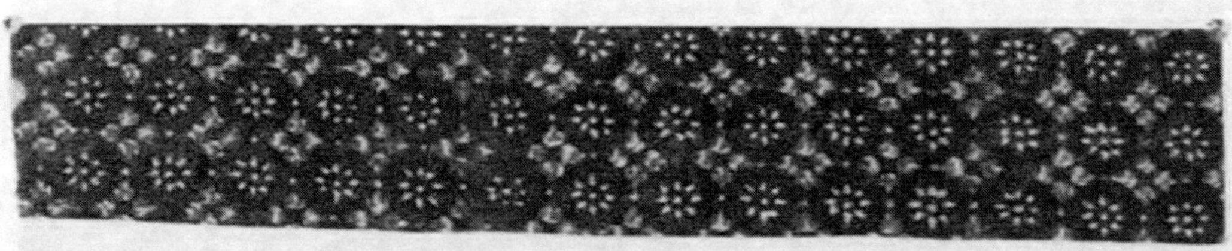

~~Prov. No. 152.~~ No. 381

INDIA FABRICS.

PIECE GOODS.

Cotton print, called "chetee" (chintz).

Length 3 yards 18 inches; width 1 yard 5 inches. Weight 1 lb. Price 2s.

From ARCOT; MADRAS.

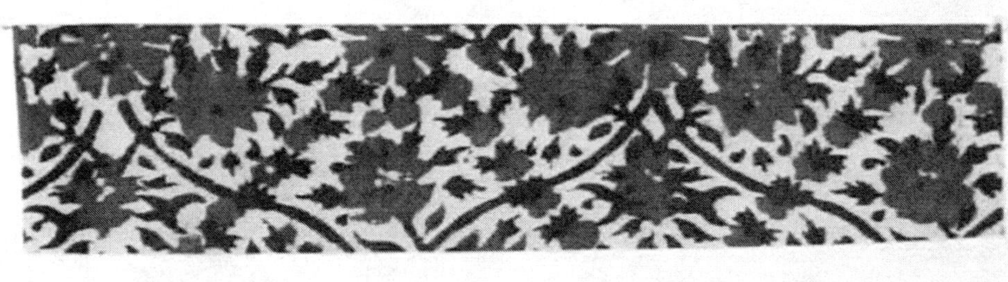

~~Prov. No. 148.~~ No. 382

INDIA FABRICS.

PIECE GOODS.

Cotton print.

Length 2 yards 18 inches ; width 1 yard. Weight 12 oz. Price 2s.

From ARCOT ; MADRAS.

~~Prov. No. 169.~~ No. 383

INDIA FABRICS.

PIECE GOODS.

Cotton print (coarse), called "chetee" (chintz).

Length 9 yards 18 inches ; width 1 yard. Weight 2 lbs. 12 oz. Price 4s. 1½d.

From PONNARY : MADRAS.

~~Prov. No. 90.~~ No. 387

INDIA FABRICS.

PIECE GOODS.

Cotton print, called "chetee" (chintz).

Length 6 yards 18 inches; width 1 yard 7 inches. Weight 1 lb. 12 oz. Price 3s. 10½d.

From PONNARY; MADRAS.

~~Pres. No. 162.~~ No. 385

INDIA FABRICS.

PIECE GOODS.

Cotton print.

Length 7 yards ; width 19 inches. Weight 1 lb. 9 oz. Price 3s. 5d.

From BELLARY ; MADRAS.

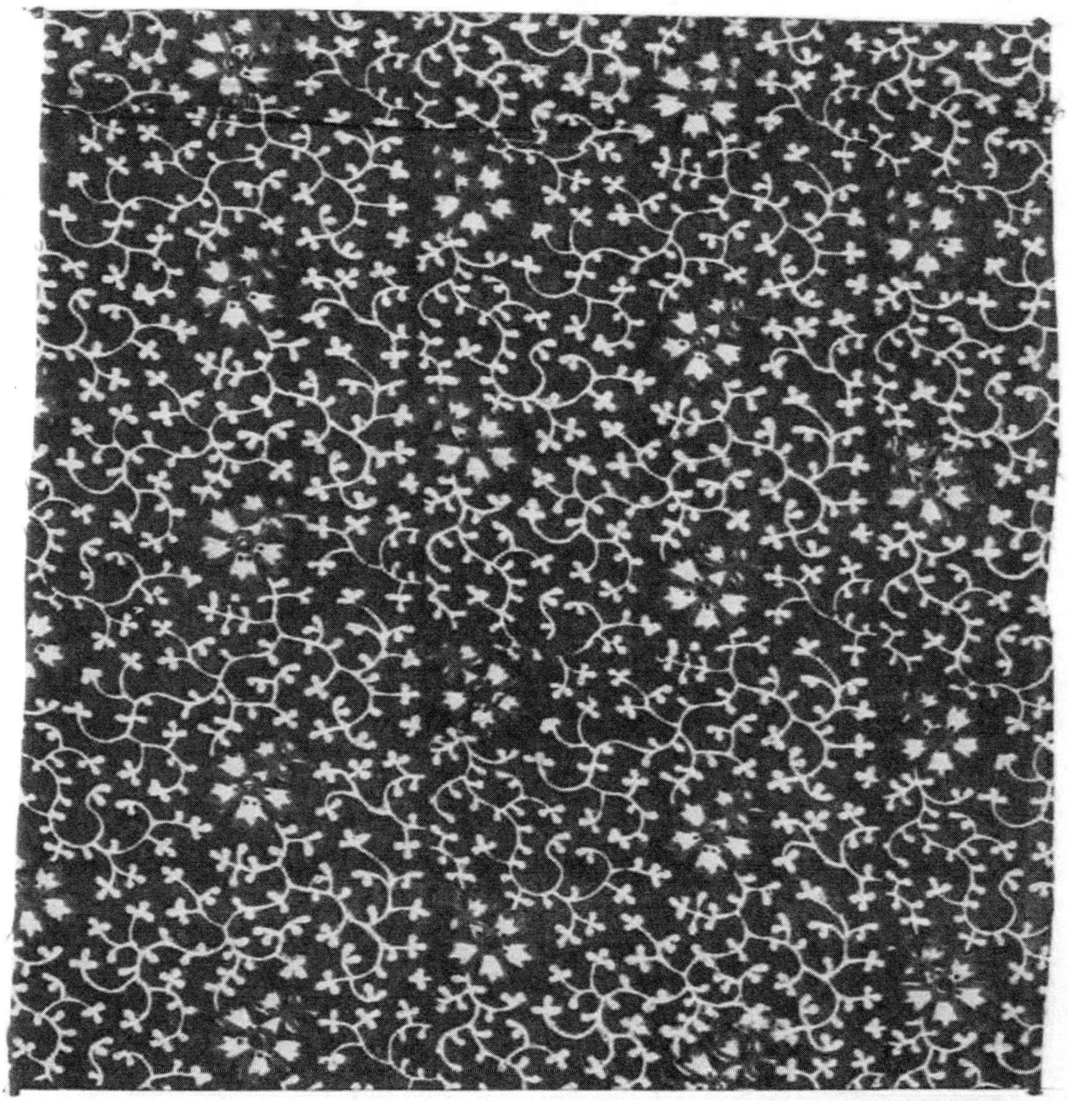

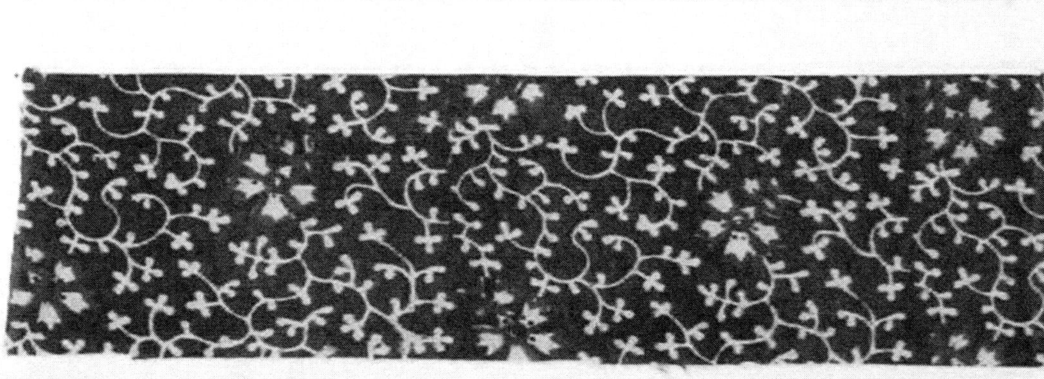

~~Paper, No. 150.~~ No. *386*

INDIA FABRICS.

PIECE GOODS.

Cotton print.

Length 4 yards; width 1 yard 6 inches. Weight 1 lb. 1 oz. Price 2s. 7½d.

From PONNARY; MADRAS.

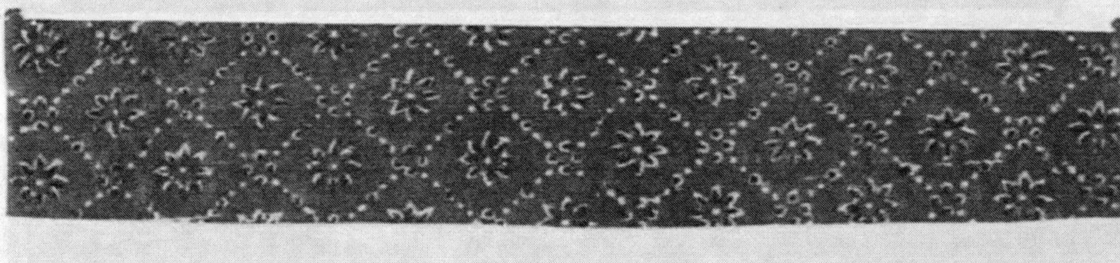

~~Prov. No. 41.~~ No. 387

INDIA FABRICS.

PIECE GOODS.

Cotton print, called "chetee" (chintz).

Length 5 yards; width 1 yard. Weight 15 oz. Price 2s.

From SYDAPAT; MADRAS.

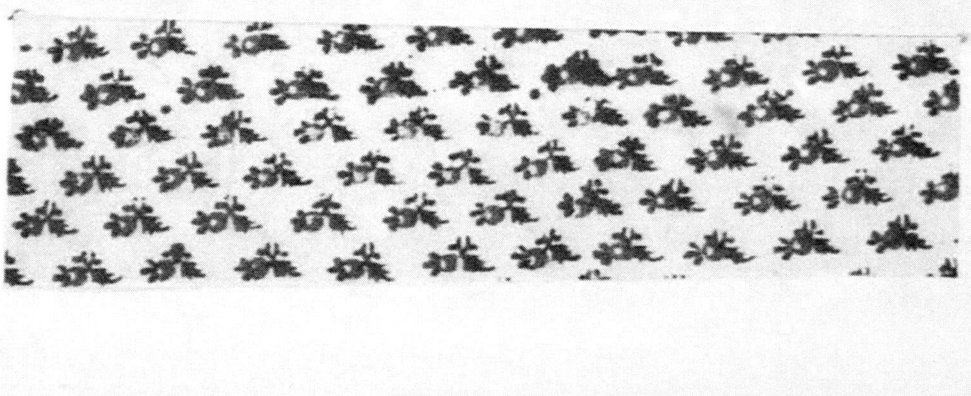

~~Prov. No. 149.~~ No. 388

INDIA FABRICS.

PIECE GOODS.

Cotton print, called "chetee" (chintz).

Length 6 yards; width 1 yard. Weight 1 lb. 5 oz. Price 4s. 6d.

From MASULIPATAM; MADRAS.

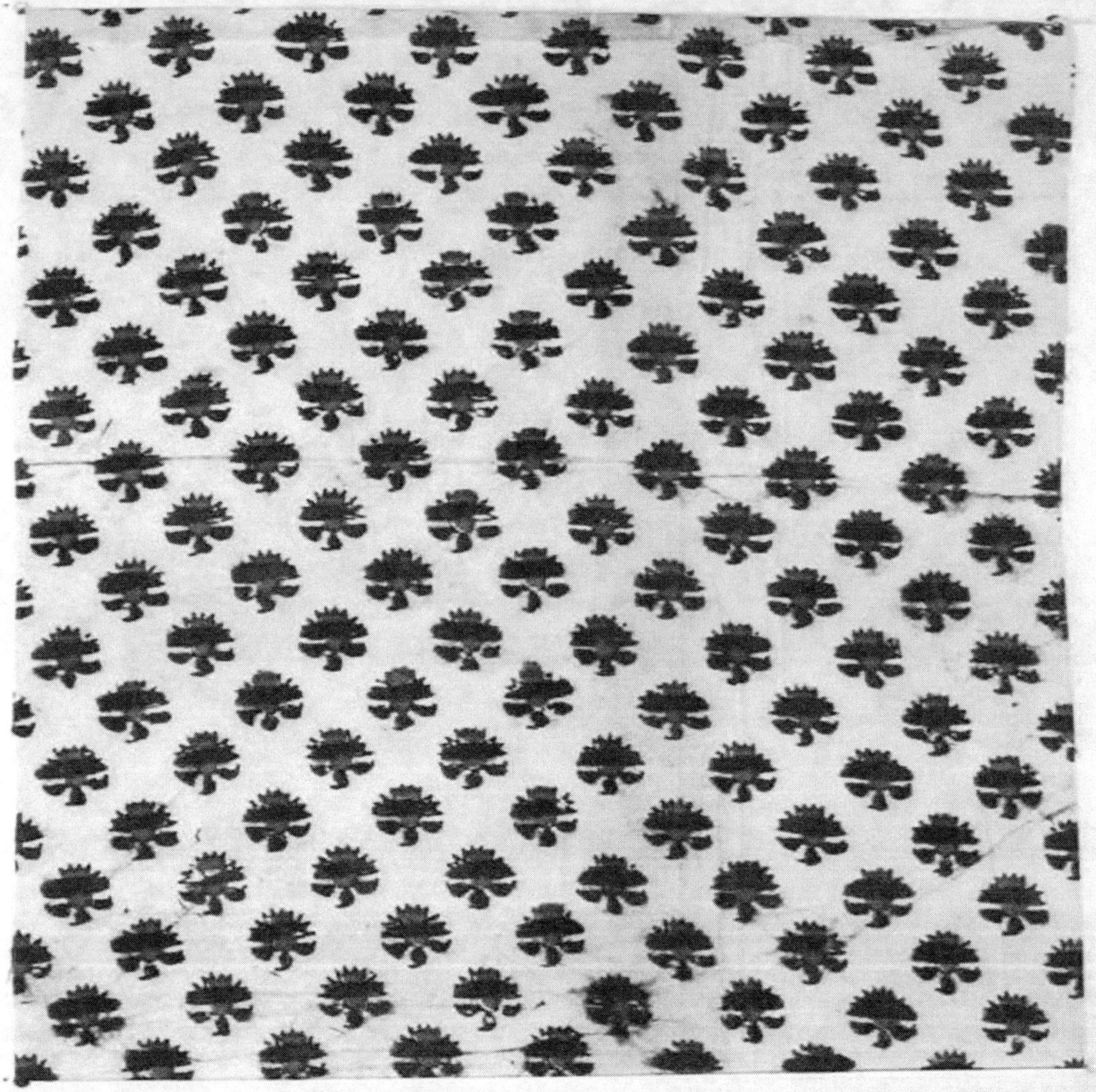

Prov. No. 151.

No. 389

INDIA FABRICS.

PIECE GOODS.

Cotton print.

Length 5 yards 18 inches; width 1 yard 6 inches. Weight 1 lb. 8 oz. Price 3s. 4½d.

From PONNARY: MADRAS.

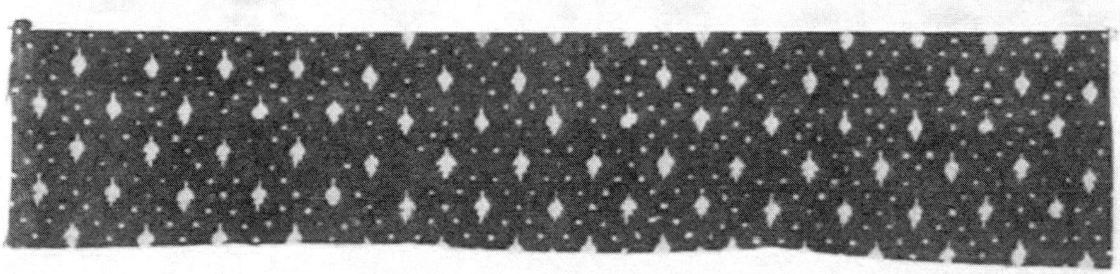

~~Prov. No. 87.~~ No. 390

INDIA FABRICS.

PIECE GOODS.

Cotton print; coarse.

Length 5 yards 27 inches; width 1 yard. Weight 1 lb. 12 oz. Price 3s. 1½d.

From MASULIPATAM; MADRAS.

~~Prov. No. 146.~~ No. 391

INDIA FABRICS.

PIECE GOODS.

Cotton print; coarse.

Length 6 yards; width 1 yard. Weight 4 lb. 12 oz. Price 3s. 1½d.

From MASULIPATAM; MADRAS.

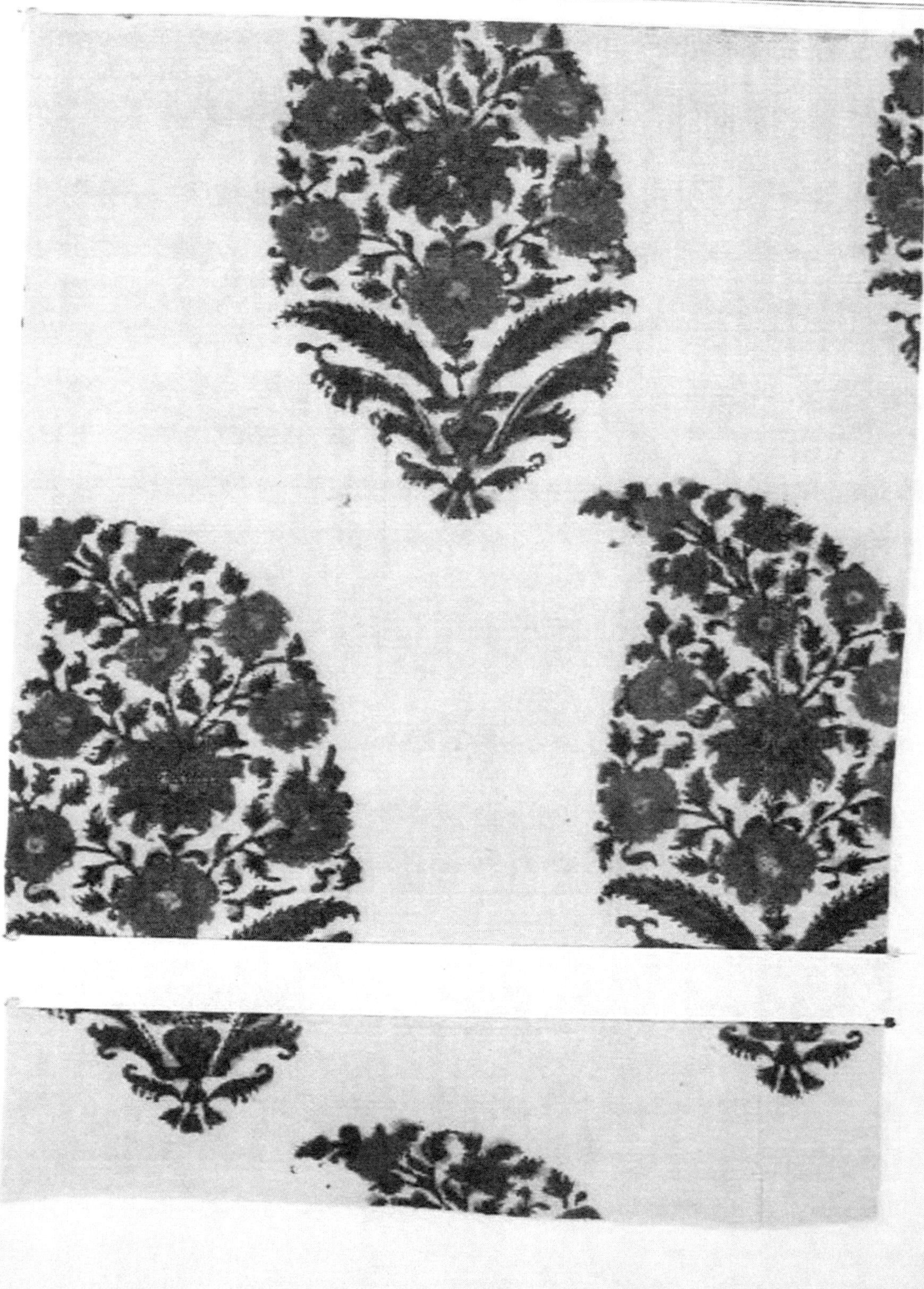

~~Prov. No. 169.~~ No. 392

INDIA FABRICS.

PIECE GOODS.

Cotton print, coarse, called "chetee" (chintz).

Length 7 yards; width 29 inches. Weight 1 lb. 9 oz. Price 2s.

From ARCOT; MADRAS.

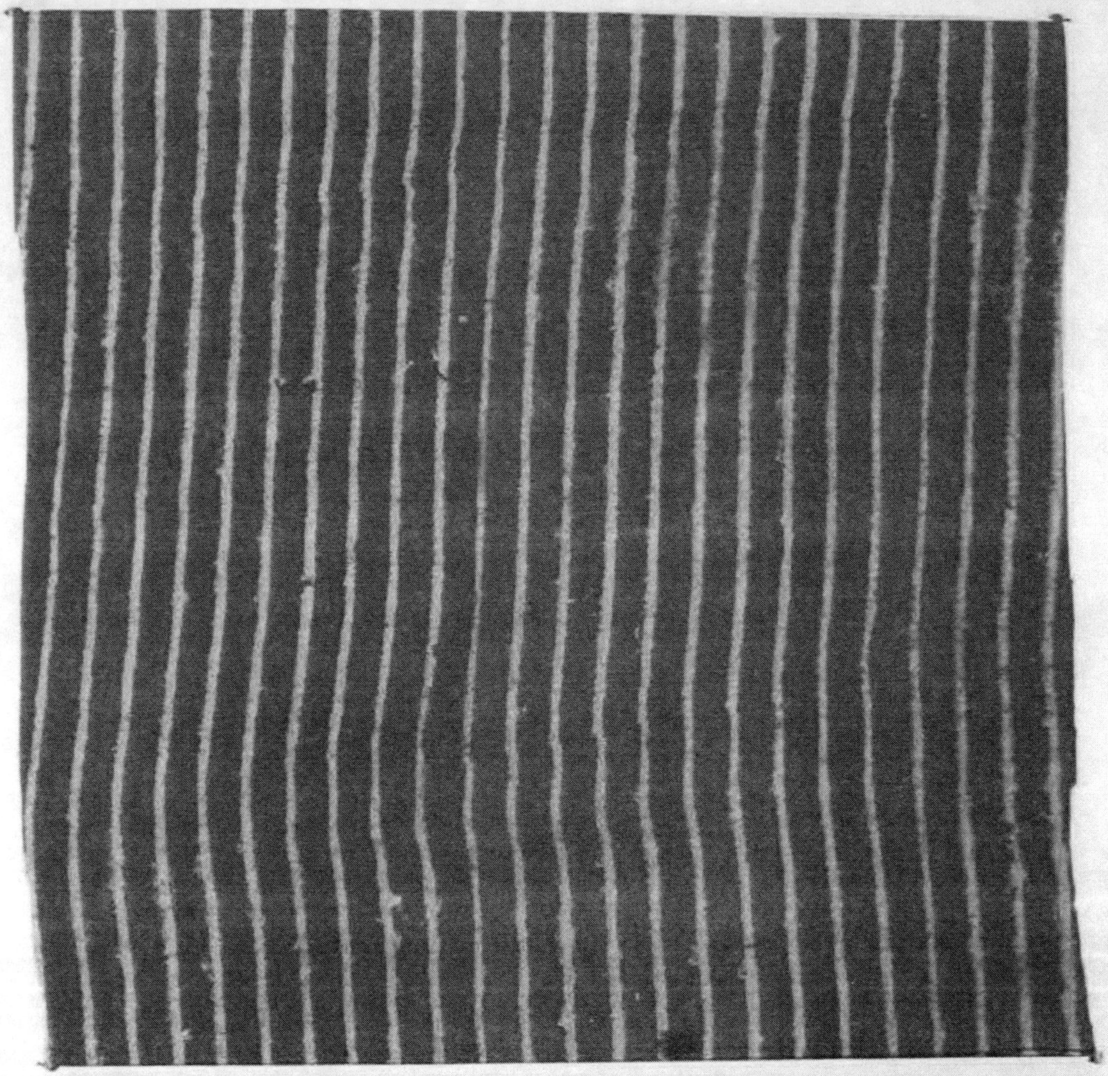

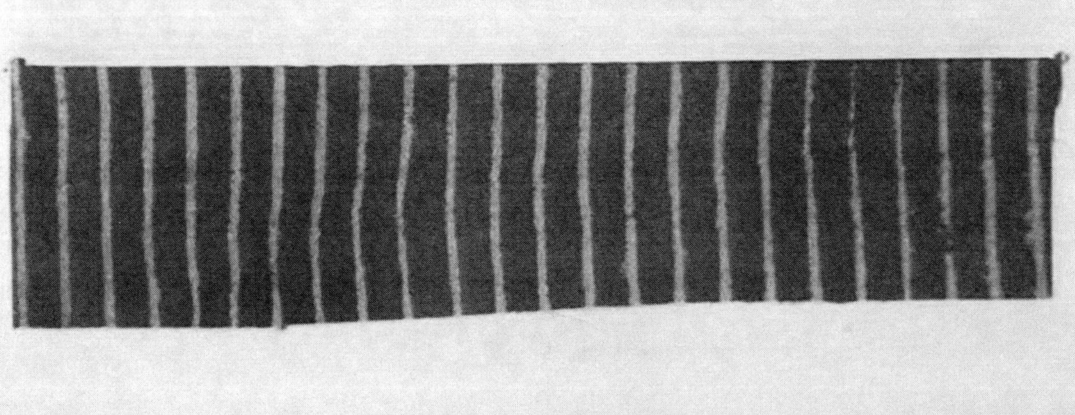

~~Prov. No. 66.~~

No. 393

INDIA FABRICS.

PIECE GOODS.

Cotton print, called "Chetee" (chintz).

PATTERN AND COLOR MUCH USED BY PARSEES.

Length 9 yards; width 1 yard 2 inches. Weight 2 lbs. 8 oz. Price 4s. 1½d.

From PONNARY; MADRAS.

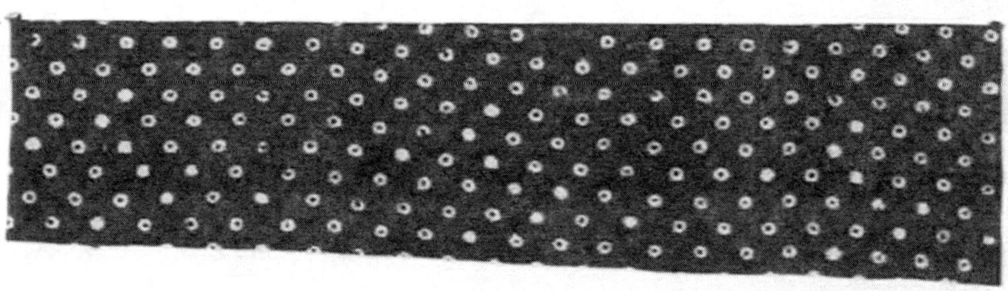

~~Prov. No. 95.~~ No. 394

INDIA FABRICS.

PIECE GOODS.

Cotton print.

THE SAME PATTERN IN SILK FROM BENARES AND HYDERABAD.

Length 7 yards; width 31 inches. Weight 1 lb. 12 oz. Price 2s. 3d.

From PONNARY; MADRAS.

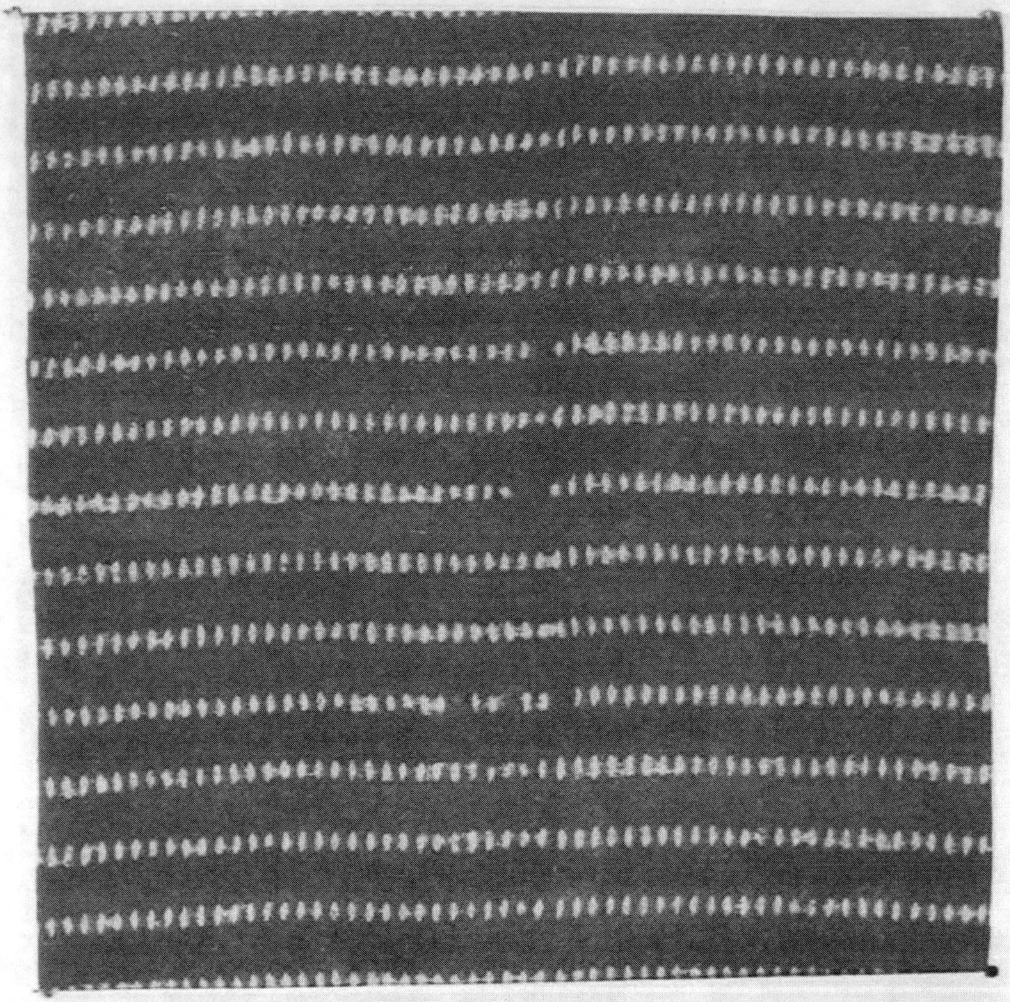

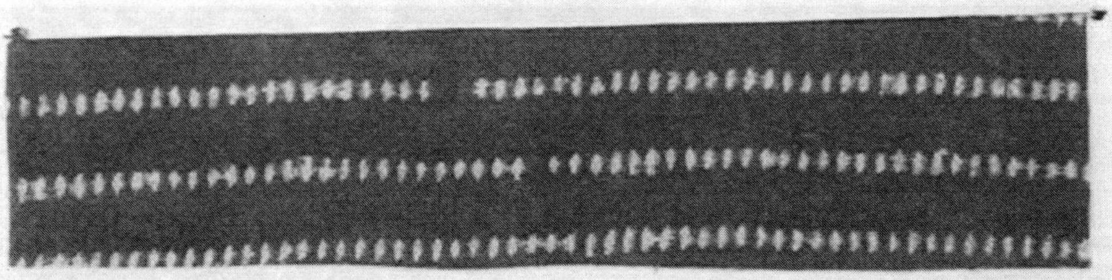

Prov. No. 91. No. 395

INDIA FABRICS.

PIECE GOODS.

Cotton print; coarse.

SAME PATTERN IN SILK FROM BENARES AND HYDERABAD.

Length 9 yards; width 1 yard. Weight 2 lbs. 10 oz. Price 4s. 1½d.

From PONNARY; MADRAS.

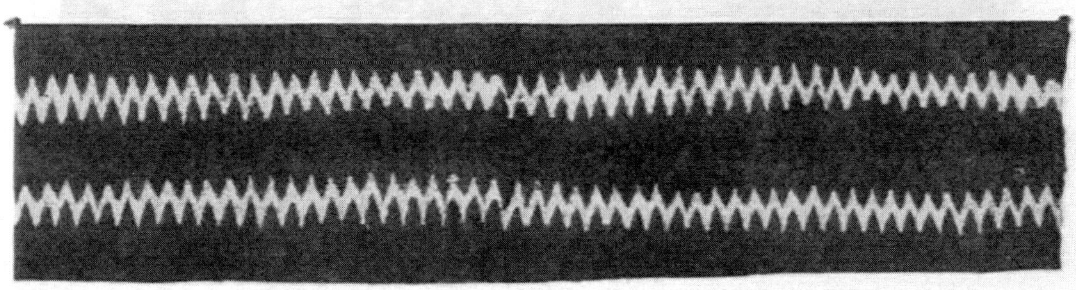

~~Prov. No. 68.~~ No. 396

INDIA FABRICS.

PIECE GOODS.

Cotton print.

SAME PATTERN IN SILK, "MUSHROOS."

Length 7 yards 9 inches; width 32 inches. Weight 1 lb. 10 oz. Price 2s. 3d.

From ARCOT; MADRAS.

Prov. No. 92. No. 397

INDIA FABRICS.

PIECE GOODS.

Cotton, called "Gud ka cheet."

WORN AS A PETTICOAT BY MALAYS OF THE POORER CLASSES.

Length 4 yards 18 inches; width 31 inches. Price 2s.

From AGRA; BENGAL.

~~Prov. No. 144.~~ No. 398

INDIA FABRICS.

PIECE GOODS.

Coarse cotton print, called "Chetee" (chintz).

USED FOR LINING TENTS.

Length 5 yards ; width 1 yard 4 inches. Weight 9 oz. Price 2s. 7½d.

From ARCOT ; MADRAS.

~~Prov. No. 145.~~ No. 399

INDIA FABRICS.

PIECE GOODS.

Cotton print, called "Chetee," (chintz).

USED FOR LINING TENTS.

Length 5 yards ; width 1 yard 4 inches. Weight 1 lb. 3 oz. Price 2s. 1½d.

From ARCOT ; MADRAS.

~~Prov. No. 149.~~ No. 400

INDIA FABRICS.

PIECE GOODS.

Cotton print, called "Chetee," (chintz).

USED FOR LINING TENTS.

Length 5 yards; width 1 yard 4 inches. Weight 1 lb. 7 oz. Price 2s. 7½d.

From ARCOT; MADRAS.

THE TEXTILE MANUFACTURERS OF INDIA

JOHN FORBES WATSON

VOLUME:-11

1866

~~Prov. No. 76.~~

No. 401

INDIA FABRICS.

PIECE GOODS.

Cotton plaid gown piece. Imitation English?

Length 6 yards; width 21 inches. Weight 13 oz. Price 3s. 10½d.

From MYLAPORE; MADRAS.

~~Prov. No. 75.~~ No. 402

INDIA FABRICS.

PIECE GOODS.

Cotton plaid gown piece. Imitation English?

Length 5 yards 27 inches; width 21 inches. Weight 13 oz. Price 3s.

From COONATOOR; MADRAS.

~~Prov. No. 902.~~ No. 1403

INDIA FABRICS.

PIECE GOODS.

Cotton gown piece.

Length 11 yards 21 inches; width 22 inches. Weight 1 lb. 3 oz. Price 5s. 6d.

From TANJORE; MADRAS.

~~Prov. No. 71.~~

No. 404

INDIA FABRICS.

PIECE GOODS.

Cotton gown piece.

Length 6 yards ; width 31 inches. Weight 12 oz. Price 5s.

From CUDDALORE; MADRAS.

~~Prov. No. 84.~~ No. 405

INDIA FABRICS.

PIECE GOODS.

Cotton check gown piece.

Length 6 yards; width 31 inches. Weight 14 oz. Price 4s. 6d.

From CUDDALORE; MADRAS.

~~Prov. No. 69.~~ No. 406

INDIA FABRICS.

PIECE GOODS.

Cotton check gown piece.

Length 5 yards 20 inches; width 26 inches. Weight 11 oz. Price 2s.

From PULICAT; MADRAS.

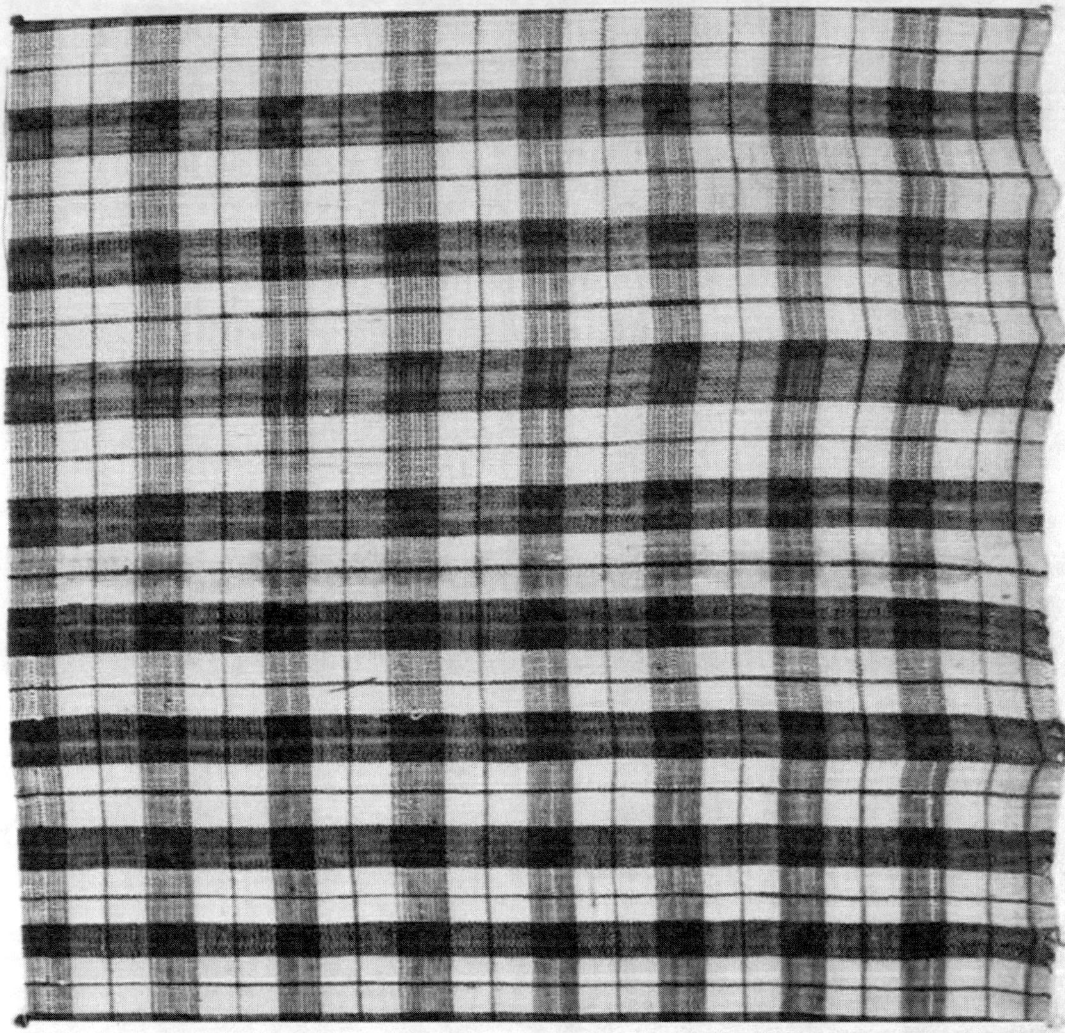

~~Prov. No. 73.~~ No. 407

INDIA FABRICS.

PIECE GOODS.

Cotton check gown piece.

Length 5 yards 23 inches; width 22 inches. Weight 14 oz. Price 4s.

From MYLAPORE; MADRAS.

~~Prov. No. 65.~~ No. 408

INDIA FABRICS.

PIECE GOODS.

Cotton gown piece.

Length 6 yards 13 inches ; width 25 inches. Weight 12 oz. 6 drs. Price 2s. 6d.

From COONATOOR ; MADRAS.

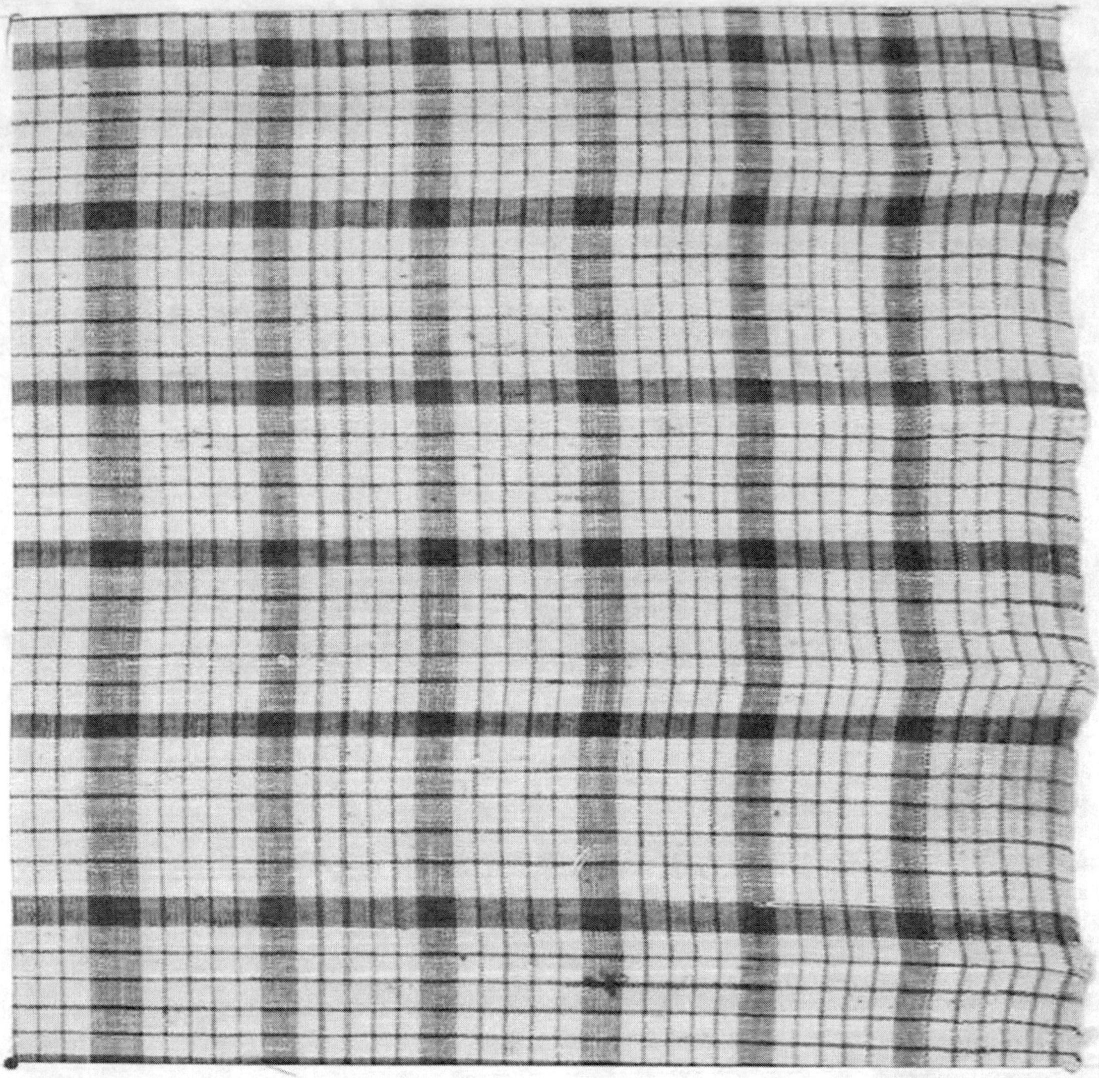

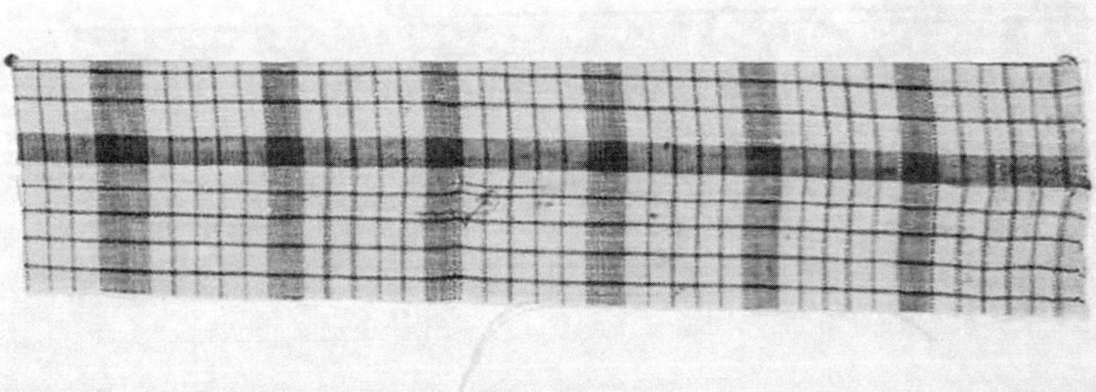

~~Paris No. 70.~~ No. 407

INDIA FABRICS.

PIECE GOODS.

Cotton small check gown piece.

Length 6 yards 8 inches; width 25 inches. Weight 12 oz. 8 drs. Price 2s. 6d.

From COONATOOR; MADRAS.

Prov. No. 66.

No. 410

INDIA FABRICS.

PIECE GOODS.

Cotton gown piece.

Lengths 7 yards 6 inches ; width 28 inches. Weight 12 oz. Price 2s. 6d.

From COONATOOR ; MADRAS.

~~Prov. No. 78.~~ No. 411

INDIA FABRICS.

PIECE GOODS.

Cotton check gown piece.

Length 6 yards 30 inches ; width 26 inches. Weight 11 oz. Price 2s. 6d.

From COONATOOR: MADRAS.

~~Prov. No. 77.~~ No. 412

INDIA FABRICS.

PIECE GOODS.

Cotton check gown piece.

Length 6 yards; width 28 inches. Weight 14 oz. Price 3s.

From PULICAT; MADRAS.

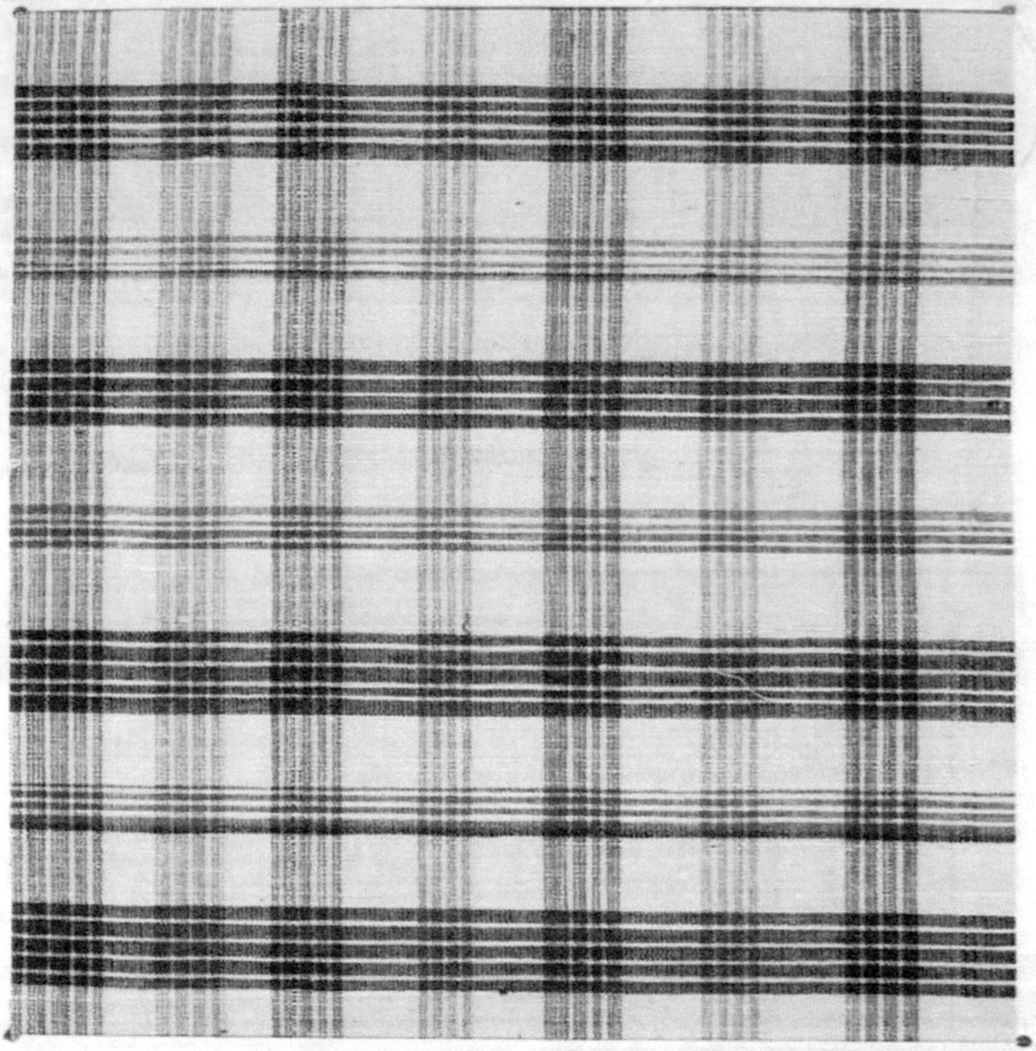

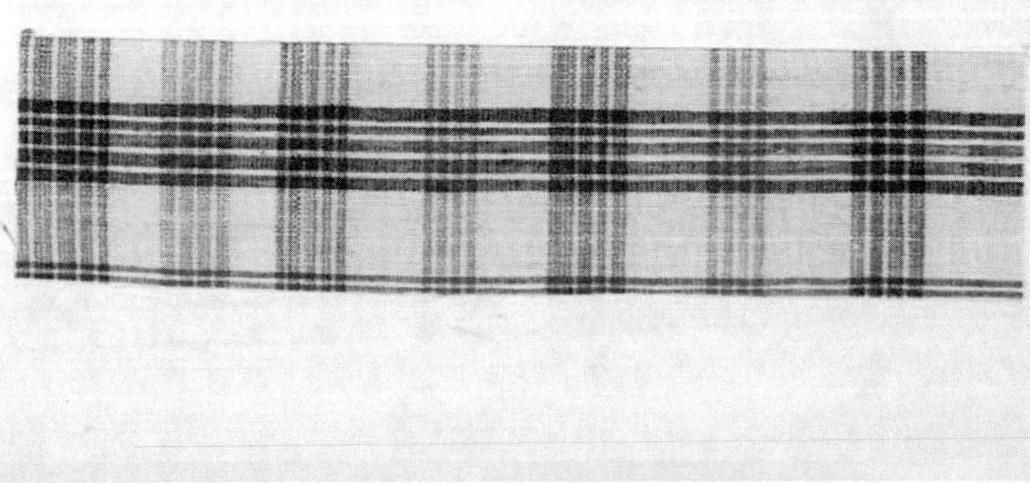

~~Prev. No. 63.~~

No. 413

INDIA FABRICS.

PIECE GOODS.

Cotton check gown piece.

Length 6 yards 26 inches; width 26 inches. Weight 15 oz. Price 4s. 6d.

From TEROOMALY; MADRAS.

~~Prov. No. 79.~~ No. 414

INDIA FABRICS.

PIECE GOODS.

Cotton check gown piece.

Length 7 yards ; width 26 inches. Weight 15 oz. Price 3s. 9d.

From COONATOOR ; MADRAS.

~~Perm. No. 72.~~ No. 4/5

INDIA FABRICS.

PIECE GOODS.

Cotton check gown piece. English pattern.

Length 6 yards 9 inches; width 18 inches. Weight 1 lb. Price 3s. 6d.

From MASULIPATAM; MADRAS.

~~Prov. No. 62.~~ No. 41b

INDIA FABRICS.

PIECE GOODS.

Small check gingham.

Length 10 yards 27 inches: width 20 inches. Weight 1 lb. 10 oz. Price 3s. 6d.

From CUDDALORE; MADRAS.

~~Prov. No. 67.~~ No. 417

INDIA FABRICS.

PIECE GOODS.

Small check gingham; good quality.

Length 6 yards; width 27 inches. Weight 1 lb. 10 oz. Price 6s.

From CUDDALORE; MADRAS.

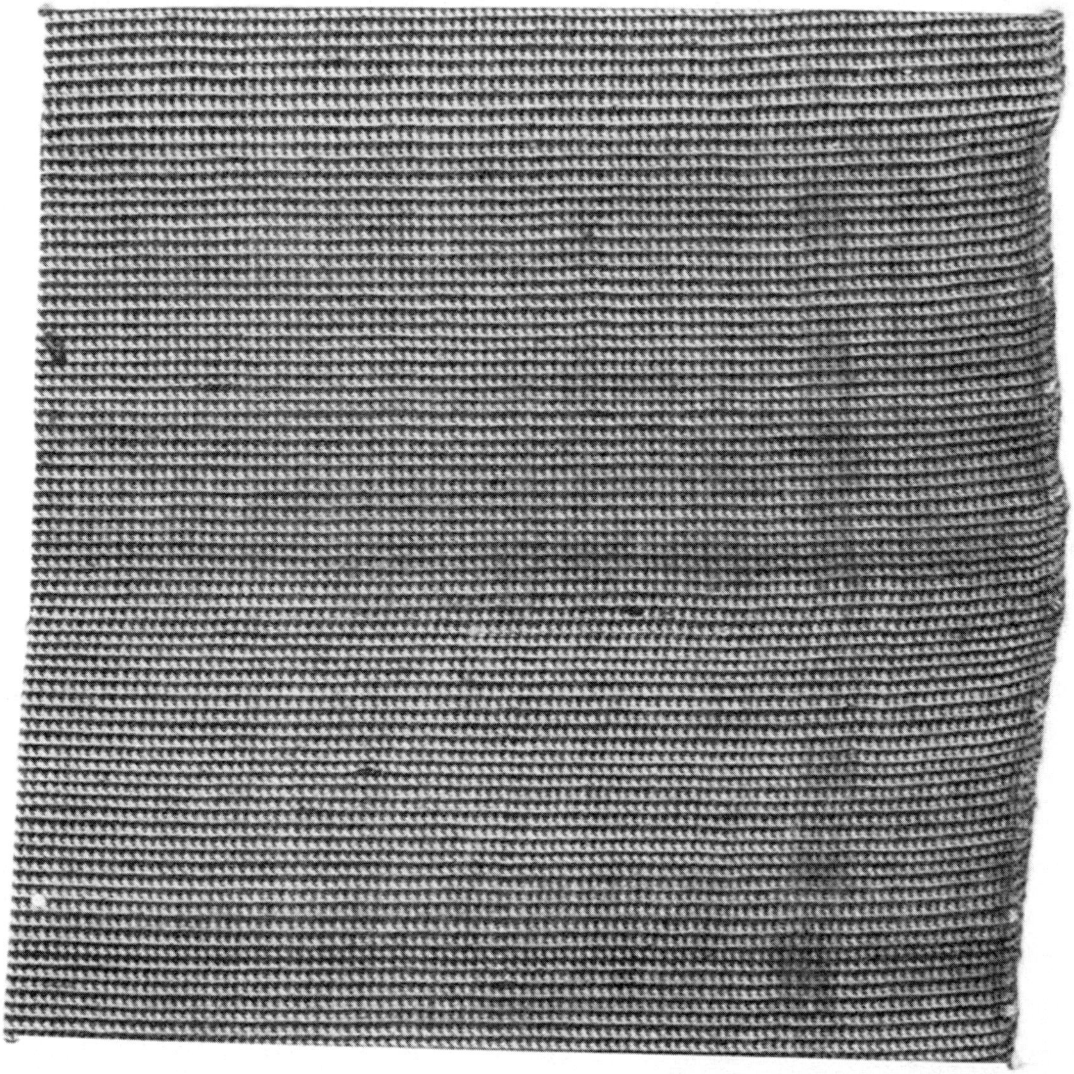

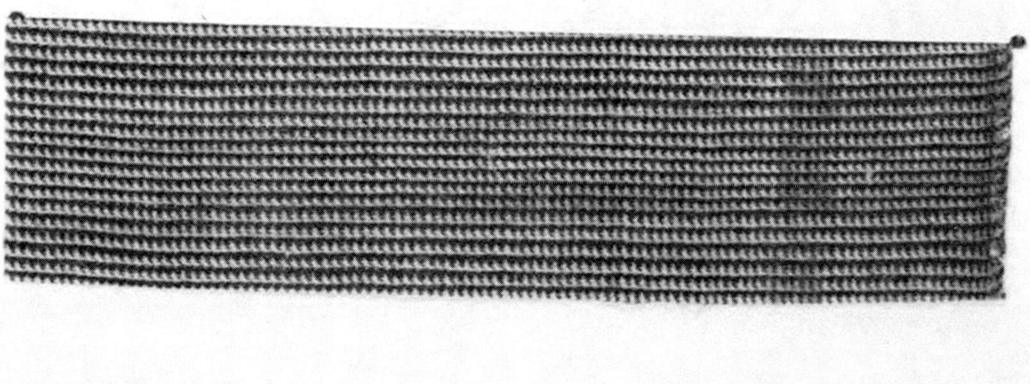

~~Prov. No. 62.~~ No. 418

INDIA FABRICS.

PIECE GOODS.

Striped gingham.

Length 10 yards; width 29 inches. Weight 2 lbs. 2 oz. Price 3s.

From PALAMCOTTAH; MADRAS.

~~Prov. No. 18.~~ No. 417

INDIA FABRICS.

TABLE NAPKINS.

Cotton (unbleached) damask napkins.

Measure 21 inches square. Price per dozen 7s.

From MADRAS.

~~Prov. No. 46~~ No. 420

INDIA FABRICS.

TABLE NAPKINS.

Cotton (unbleached) damask napkins.

Measure 19 inches square. Price per dozen 8s.

From CUDDALORE; MADRAS.

~~Prov. No. 17.~~ No. 421

INDIA FABRICS.

TABLE NAPKINS.

Cotton (unbleached) diaper napkins.

Measure 22 inches square. Price per dozen 8s. 6d.

From CUDDALORE; MADRAS.

~~Parr. No. 60.~~ No. 422

INDIA FABRICS.

TOWELS.

Cotton (unbleached) huckaback towels.

35 inches square. Price per dozen 13*s*.

From CUDDALORE; MADRAS.

~~Prov. No. 49.~~ No. 423

INDIA FABRICS.

TOWELS.

Cotton (bleached) dungary towels.

Length 33 inches; width 22 inches. Price per dozen 4s.

From CUDDALORE; MADRAS.

~~Prov. No. 51.~~ No. 424

INDIA FABRICS.

TABLE NAPKINS.

Cotton (unbleached) damask napkins.

Length 30 inches by 29 inches. Price 13s. per dozen.

From MASULIPATAM; MADRAS.

~~Prov. No. 52.~~ No. 425

INDIA FABRICS.

TOWELS.

Cotton (unbleached) diaper towels.

Length 36 inches; width 31 inches. Price per dozen 8s.

From CHINGLEPUT; MADRAS.

~~Prov. No. 58.~~ No. 42 *b*

INDIA FABRICS.

TABLE NAPKINS.

Cotton (bleached) diaper napkins.

Measure 17 inches square. Price per dozen 2*s.* 3*d.*

From MASULIPATAM; MADRAS.

~~Prov. No. 31.~~ No. 427

INDIA FABRICS.

TOWELS.

Cotton (unbleached) dungary towels.

Length 32 inches; width 31 inches. Price per dozen 4s.

From SALEM; MADRAS.

~~Prov. No. 55.~~ No. 428

INDIA FABRICS.

TABLE NAPKINS.

Cotton (unbleached) damask napkins.

Measure 23 inches square. Price per dozen 5s.

From BROACH; BOMBAY.

~~Prov. No. 56.~~

No. 429

INDIA FABRICS.

TOWELS.

Cotton (coarse) unbleached huckaback towels.

Measure 33 inches square. Price per dozen 2*s.* 3*d.*

From BROACH; BOMBAY.

~~Proof No. 173.~~ No. 430

INDIA FABRICS.

TOWELS.

Cotton hand towels, (like diaper,) coloured borders.

Length 27 inches; width 25 inches. Price per dozen 3s. Made to order.

From GOA; *sent from* MADRAS.

~~Prov. No. 175.~~

No. 431

INDIA FABRICS.

DOYLEYS.

Cotton doyleys in colors.

Measure 13 inches square. Price per dozen 9s.

From MADRAS.

~~Prov. No. 174.~~

No. 432

INDIA FABRICS.

DOYLEYS.

Cotton doyley in colors.

Measure 13 inches square. Price per dozen 8s. 3d.

From CUDDALORE; MADRAS.

~~Prov. No. 603.~~

No. 433

INDIA FABRICS.

Cotton "Soojnee" or counterpane (quilted).

Length 2 yards 6 inches; width 1 yard 10 inches. Weight 2 lbs. 4 oz. Price 8s.

From HYDERABAD; DECCAN.

~~Prov. No. 504.~~ No. 434

INDIA FABRICS.

RUGS.

Cotton sleeping rug; sewn together in centre.

Length 2 yards 8 inches; width 1 yard 24 inches. Weight 6 lbs. 2 oz.

From UPPER ASSAM.

~~Prov. No. 935.~~ No. 435

INDIA FABRICS.

RUGS.

Cotton "Suttringee" or rug.

Length 1 yard 32 inches; width 32 inches. Weight 2 lbs. 4 oz. Price 3s.

From MANGALORE; MADRAS.

~~Prov. No. 60.~~ No. 436

INDIA FABRICS.

RUGS.

Cotton "Suttringee" or sleeping rug.

Length 5 yards 13 inches; width 2 yards 20 inches. Weight 15 lbs. 3 oz. Price 2s.

From MANGALORE; MADRAS.

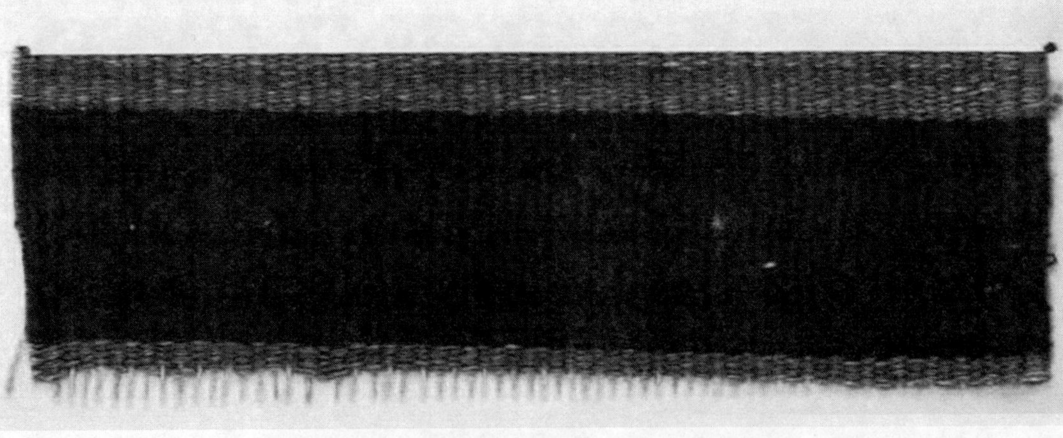

~~Room No. 974.~~

No. 437

INDIA FABRICS.

RUGS.

Cotton "Suttringee" or rug.

SEPOY REGULATION RUG.

Length 2 yards 14 inches; width 1 yard 4 inches. Weight 2 lbs. 2 oz. Price 2s.

From PALAMCOTTAH; MADRAS.

~~Prov. No. 69.~~ No. 438

INDIA FABRICS.

RUGS.

Cotton "Suttringee" or Rug.

Length 2 yards 16 inches; width 1 yard 6½ inches. Weight 2 lbs. 14 oz. Price 2s.

From PALAMCOTTAH; MADRAS.

~~Prov. No. 595.~~

No. 437

INDIA FABRICS.

RUGS.

Cotton "Suttringee" or rug.

VERY DURABLE FABRIC.

Length 2 yards 30 inches; width 1 yard 24 inches. Weight 8 lbs. 11 oz.

From AGRA; BENGAL.

~~Peon. No. 506.~~ No. 440

INDIA FABRICS.

RUGS.

Cotton "Suttringee" or rug.

VERY DURABLE FABRIC.

Length 2 yards 30 inches; width 1 yard 19 inches. Weight 8 lbs. 13 oz.

From AGRA; BENGAL.

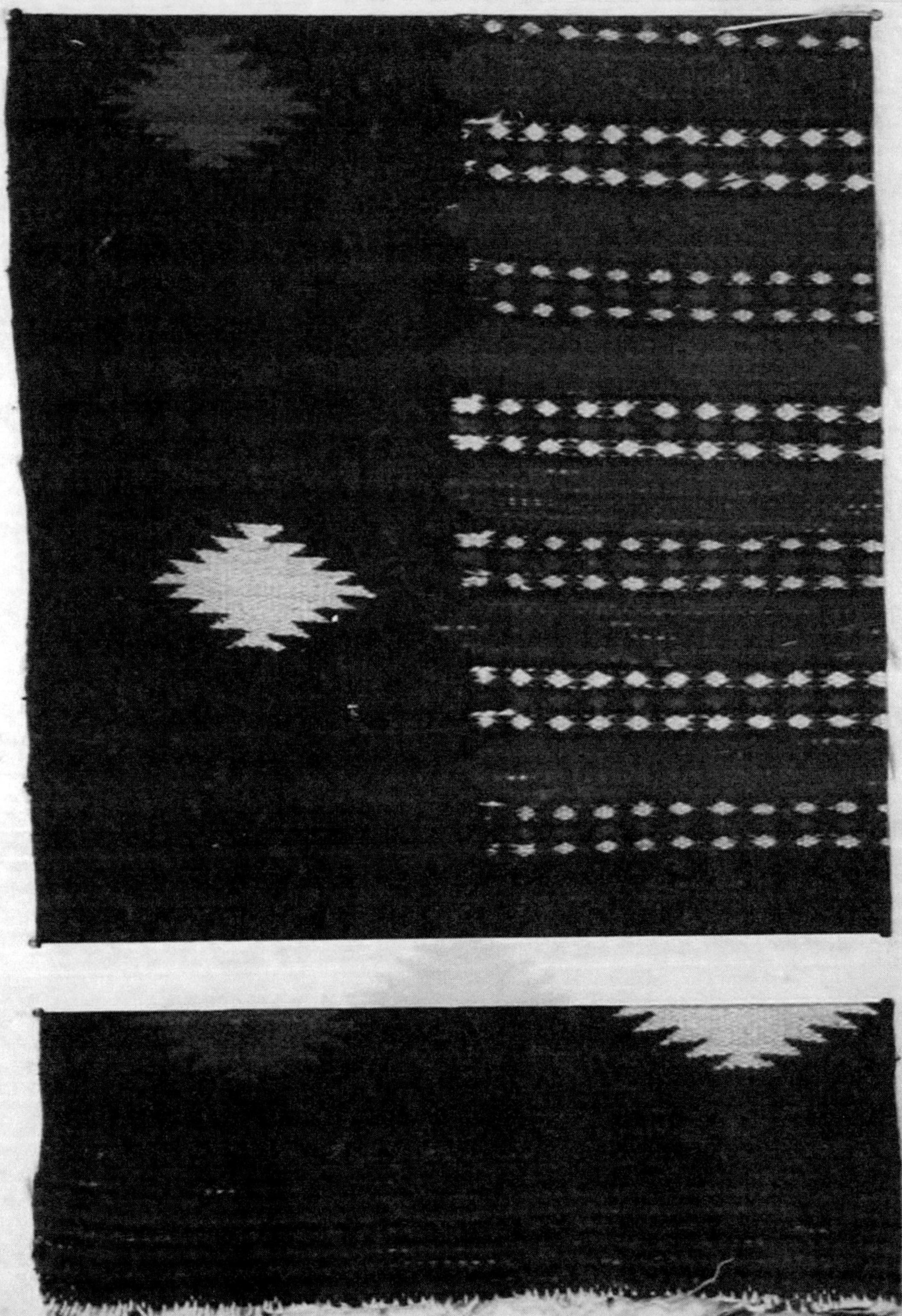

THE TEXTILE MANUFACTURERS OF INDIA

JOHN FORBES WATSON

VOLUME:-12

1866

~~Prev. No. 912~~ No. 441

INDIA FABRICS.

PIECE GOODS.

Silk ~~and cotton~~, with gold stripes.

For making up into "Cholees," a kind of tight-fitting jacket or bodice for women; material for six Cholees, woven with "fag" between, constitute one piece.

Length of single portion 17 inches; width 29 inches. Weight 1¼ oz. Price 1*s.* 9*d.*

From TANJORE; MADRAS.

~~Prov. No. 914.~~

No. 442

INDIA FABRICS.

PIECE GOODS.

Silk ~~and cotton~~, with silver stripes.

Used for making up into "Cholees," a kind of tight fitting jacket or bodice for women. Six in a piece.

Length of single piece 17 inches; width 29 inches. Weight $1\frac{1}{2}$ oz. Price 1s. 9d.

From TANJORE; MADRAS.

~~Prov. No. 213.~~ No. 443

INDIA FABRICS.

PIECE GOODS.

Silk ~~and cotton~~ with silver stripes.

Used for making up into "Cholees," a kind of tight-fitting jacket or bodice. Six in a piece.

Length of single piece 17 inches; width 29 inches. Weight 1¼ oz. Price 1s. 9d.

From TANJORE; MADRAS.

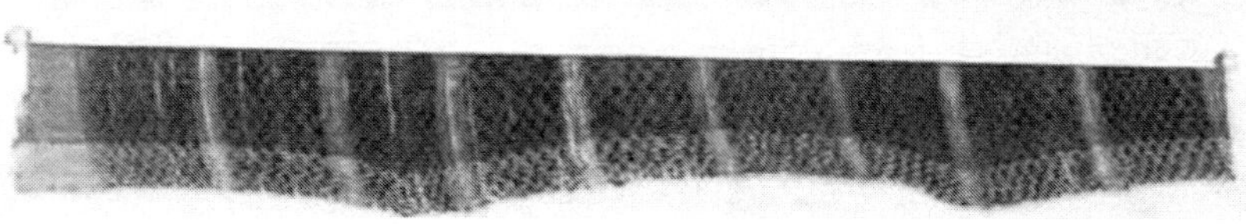

~~Prev. No. 915~~. No. 444

INDIA FABRICS.

PIECE GOODS.

Silk and cotton in colored stripes.

Used for making up into "Cholees," a kind of bodice or tight-fitting jacket for women. Six in a piece.

Length of single portion 24 inches; width 19 inches. Weight $1\frac{1}{2}$ oz. Price 1*s*. 9*d*.

From TRICHINOPOLY; MADRAS.

~~Prov. No. 138.~~ No. 445

INDIA FABRICS.

PIECE GOODS.

Silk gauze with gold flowers and borders.

For making up into "Cholees," a kind of tight-fitting jacket or bodice for women.

Length 22 inches; width 1 yard 7 inches. Price 13s.

From HYDERABAD; *bought in* MADRAS.

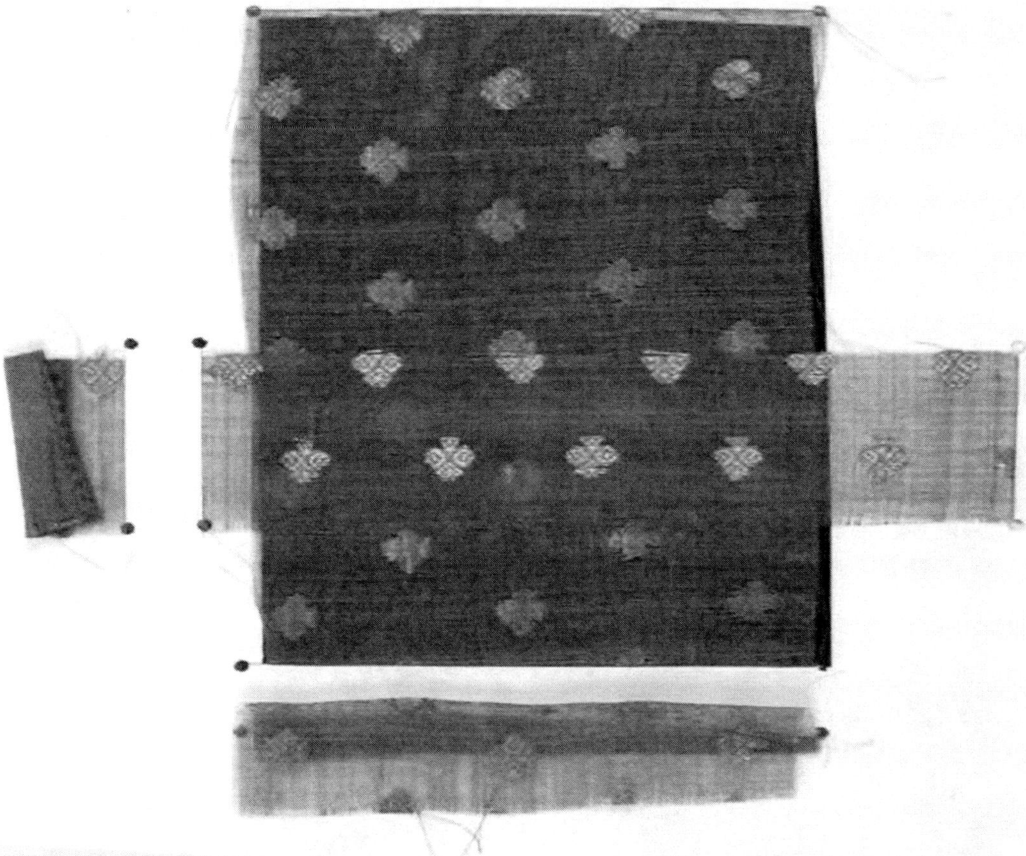

No. 444

INDIA FABRICS.

PIECE GOODS.

Cotton and silk gauze. Used for petticoats.

Length of piece 7 yards; width 23 inches. Weight 13 oz. Price 14s.

From TRICHINOPOLY; MADRAS.

~~Prov. No. 282.~~

No. 447

INDIA FABRICS.

PIECE GOODS.

Cotton and silk. Used for petticoats.

Length of piece 11 yards 15 inches; width 23 inches. Weight 14⅝ oz. Price 10s.

From TANJORE; MADRAS.

~~Prov. No. 207.~~ No. 440

INDIA FABRICS.

PIECE GOODS.

Cotton and silk. Material called "Soosee."

USED FOR TROUSERING BY MAHOMEDANS OF BOTH SEXES.

Length 7 yards; width 32 inches. Weight 14 oz. Price 8s.

From TRICHINOPOLY; MADRAS.

~~Prov. No. 266.~~ No. 447

INDIA FABRICS.

PIECE GOODS.

Cotton and silk. Material called "Soosee."

USED FOR PETTICOATS AND ALSO FOR TROUSERS.

Length 8 yards; width 1 yard. Weight 15 oz. Price 8s.

From SYEMPETTAH; MADRAS.

~~Prov. No. 208.~~ No. 450

INDIA FABRICS.

PIECE FABRIC.

Cotton. Material called "Soosee."

USED FOR TROUSERINGS AND PETTICOATS BY MAHOMEDANS OF BOTH SEXES.

Length 6 yards; width 26 inches. Weight 10 oz. Price 2s.

From SYEMPETTAH; MADRAS.

~~Prov. No. 208.~~ No. 457

INDIA FABRICS.

PIECE GOODS.

Cotton and silk, material called "Soosee."

USED FOR PETTICOATS AND TROUSERING BY MAHOMEDANS OF BOTH SEXES.

Length 7 yards ; width 33 inches. Weight 12 oz. Price 8s.

From TRICHINOPOLY ; MADRAS.

~~Prov. No. 196.~~

No. 452

INDIA FABRICS.

PIECE GOODS.

Silk and cotton, material called "Soosee."

USED FOR TROUSERING.

Length 11 yards; width 27 inches. Weight 1 lb. 9 oz. Price 8s.

From TRICHINOPOLY; MADRAS.

~~Prov. No. 63.~~ No. 453

INDIA FABRICS.

PIECE GOODS.

Cotton, material called "Soosee."

USED FOR PETTICOATS AND TROUSERS BY MAHOMEDANS OF BOTH SEXES.

Length 6 yards; width 29 inches. Weight 15 oz. Price 2s. 4½d.

From COONATOOR; MADRAS.

~~Prov. No. 59.~~ No. 454

INDIA FABRICS.

PIECE GOODS.

Cotton check.

ENGLISH PATTERN.

Length 8 yards; width 32 inches. Weight 2 lbs. 5 oz. Price 5s. 2d.

From MASULIPATAM; MADRAS.

~~Prov. No. 61.~~ No. 455

INDIA FABRICS.

PIECE GOODS.

Cotton twill for trowsering.

Length 5 yards 11 inches; width 25 inches. Weight 1 lb. 10 oz. Price 4s. 1½d.

From CUDDALORE; MADRAS.

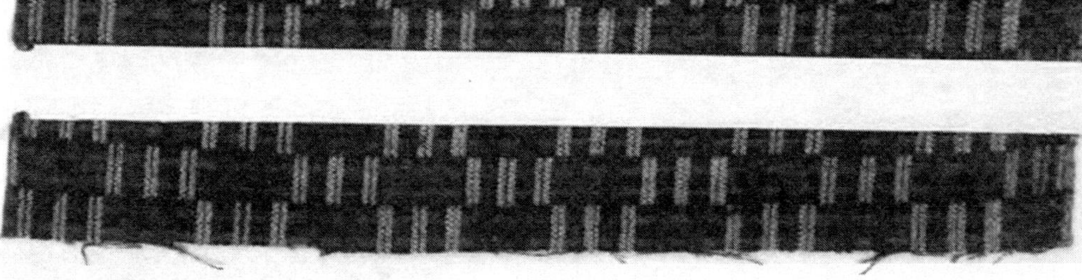

~~Prov. No. 60.~~ No. 456

INDIA FABRICS.

PIECE GOODS.

Cotton twill for trowsering.

Lengths 5 yards 12 inches; width 22 inches. Weight 1 lb. 10 oz. Price 2s. 6d.

From CUDDALORE; MADRAS.

~~Prov. No. 141.~~ No. 457

INDIA FABRICS.

PLAIN POCKET HANDKERCHIEFS.

Cotton; deep borders.

Measurement 20 inches square. Price per dozen 4s. 6d.

From NELLORE; MADRAS.

~~Proof No. 142.~~ No. 458

INDIA FABRICS.

COTTON.

Plain cotton pocket handkerchiefs; deep borders.

Measurement 20 inches square. Price per dozen 8s.

From NELLORE; MADRAS.

~~Prov. No. 140.~~ No. 457

INDIA FABRICS.

COTTON.

Chunderkhana muslin, (2d quality,) or handkerchief cloth.

WITHOUT BORDERS. OF GOOD QUALITY.

Length 8 yards; width 1 yard 2 inches. Weight 12 oz. Price 18s.

From ARNEE; MADRAS.

~~Prov No. 135.~~ No. 440

INDIA FABRICS.

COTTON.

Plain muslin fabric.

SIMILAR TO DACCA MUSLIN FROM ITS SOFTNESS OF TEXTURE.

Length 12 yards ; width 1 yard 3 inches. Weight 11 oz. 8 drs. Price 12s.

From HYDERABAD, DECCAN ; *bought in* MADRAS.

~~Prov. No. 100.~~ No. 461

INDIA FABRICS.

COTTON.

Colored cotton kerchiefs; coarse.

Measures of the two sizes manufactured : 1st size 23 inches square ; 2nd size 27 inches square. Price of largest size 1s. 6d. each.

From CUNDAPOOR IN CANARA.

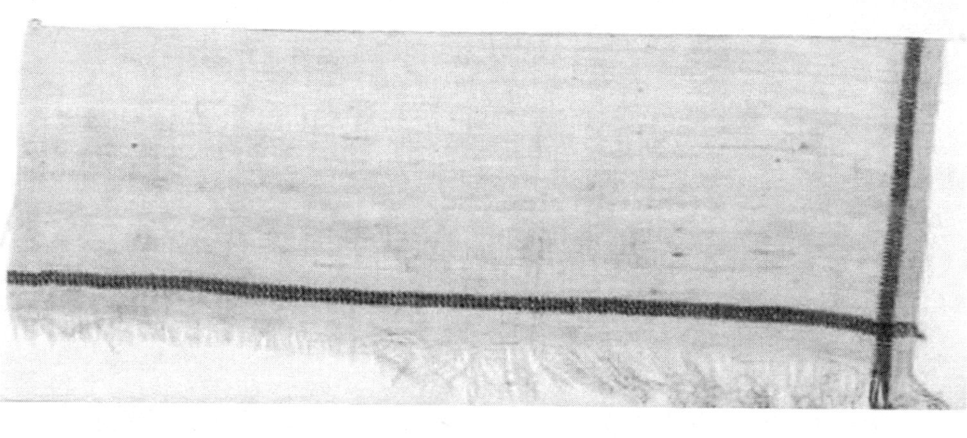

~~Pace No. 110.~~ No. 462

INDIA FABRICS.

COTTON.

Cotton kerchief, with colored borders.

Measurement 29 inches square. Weight of eight together 1 lb. 1 oz. Price of eight 4s. 6d.

From MASULIPATAM; MADRAS.

~~Prov. No. 179.~~ No. 443

INDIA FABRICS.

LONG CLOTH.

Cotton; fine quality. Made to order.

Length 33 yards ——, width 1 yard —— Weight 4 lbs. 14 ozs. Price 8/ —

From RAJAHMUNDRY; MADRAS.

~~Proy. No. 180.~~ No. 464

INDIA FABRICS.

LONG CLOTH.

Calico of good quality, called "watered Isree."

Length 11 yards 24 inches; width 1 yard. Weight 2 lbs. 4 oz. Price 1*l.* 6*s.*

From NELLORE; MADRAS.

~~Piece No. 176.~~ No. 465

INDIA FABRICS.

LONG CLOTH.

Plain: coarse, called "Isree."

Length 6 yards 18 inches; width 31 inches. Weight 1 lb. 12 oz. Price 4s.

From VIZAGAPATAM; MADRAS.

~~Prov. No. 177~~. No. 466

INDIA FABRICS.

"PUNJUM" CLOTH 22's.

Calico of coarse quality, called in India "Punjum."

Length 10 yards 9 inches; width 1 yard 4 inches. Weight 2 lbs. 5 oz. Price 7s.

From NELLORE; MADRAS.

~~Piece No. 178.~~ No. 467

INDIA FABRICS.

"PUNJUM" CLOTH 20's.

Calico of coarse quality.

Length 18 yards 18 inches; width 1 yard 2 inches. Weight 4 lbs. 14 oz. Price 18s.

From VIZAGAPATAM; MADRAS.

~~Prov. No. 181.~~ No. 468

INDIA FABRICS.

PIECE GOODS.

Cotton canvas (bleached).

Length 12 yards ; width 30 inches. Weight 5 lbs. Price 7s.

From NELLORE ; MADRAS.

~~Prov. No. 111.~~ No. 469

INDIA FABRICS.

COTTON.

Dimity, figured, unbleached. Called "Soojney."

USED FOR SHEETING.

Length 3 yards; width 1 yard 17 inches. Weight 1 lb. 14 oz. Price 6s. 3d.

From MADRAS.

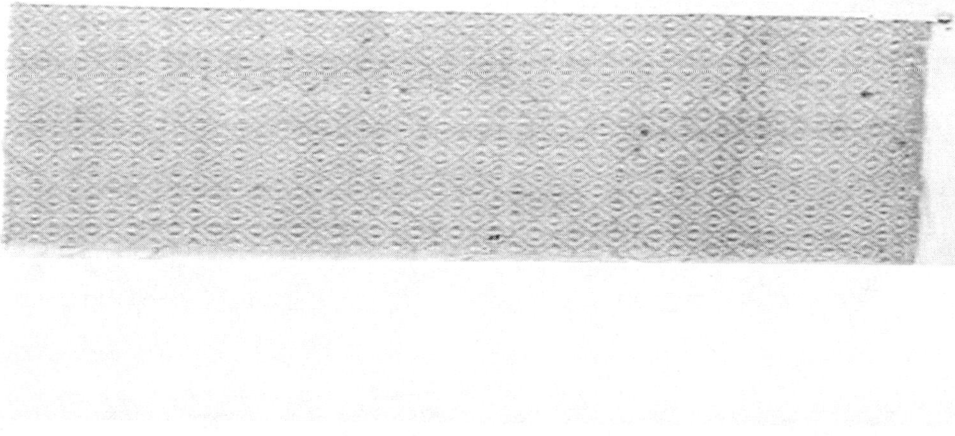

~~Prov. No. 109.~~ No. 470

INDIA FABRICS.

COTTON.

"Punjum" cloth. Unbleached; coarse.

Length (incomplete) 35 yards; width 1 yard. Price 9s. 6d.

From VIZAGAPATAM; MADRAS.

~~Prov. No. 103.~~ No. 471

INDIA FABRICS.

COTTON.

" Dungary " cloth ; unbleached. (Incomplete piece.)

Width 15½ inches.

From SALEM ; MADRAS.

No. 471. A.

INDIAN FABRICS.

COTTON.

Tent cloth.

From JUBBULPORE.

~~Parr. No. 231~~. No. 472

INDIA FABRICS.

COTTON.

Country canvas; unbleached.

Length 19 yards; width 23 inches. Weight 10 lbs. 11 oz. Price 9s. 6d.

From RAJAHMUNDRY; MADRAS.

~~Prov. No. 105.~~ No. 473

INDIA FABRICS.

COTTON.

"Dungary" cloth. Used as sail cloth.

Length 16 yards; width 23 inches. Weight 6 lbs. 10 ozs. Price 6s.

From SALEM; MADRAS.

~~Piece No. 104.~~ No. 4/4

INDIA FABRICS.

COTTON.

"Dungary" cloth; coarse.

Length 11 yards; width 23 inches. Weight 2 lbs. 6 oz. Price 2s.

From SALEM; MADRAS.

~~Poon No. 122.~~ No. 475

INDIA FABRICS.

CHINTZES.

Small glazed "Palampore" or bed-covering.

FOUR WOVEN IN ONE PIECE.

Measurement 1 yard 12 inches square. Weight of four 1 lb. 7 oz. Price of four 14s., or 2s. 6d. each.

From MASULIPATAM; MADRAS.

~~Prov. No. 105.~~ No. 416

INDIA FABRICS.

CHINTZES (UNGLAZED).

"Palampore" (bed cover).

COTTON PRINTED, PINE-PATTERN ENDS. SEWN TOGETHER IN CENTRE.

Length 2 yards 9 inches; width 1 yard 23 inches. Weight 13 oz. Price 1*s.* 5*d.*

From PAUMODEE; MADRAS.

~~Prov. No. 147.~~ No. 477

INDIA FABRICS.

CHINTZES (UNGLAZED).

"Palampore" or bed cover.

PRINTED COTTON.

Length 2 yards; width 1 yard. Weight 8 oz. Price 1s. 3d.

From MASULIPATAM; MADRAS.

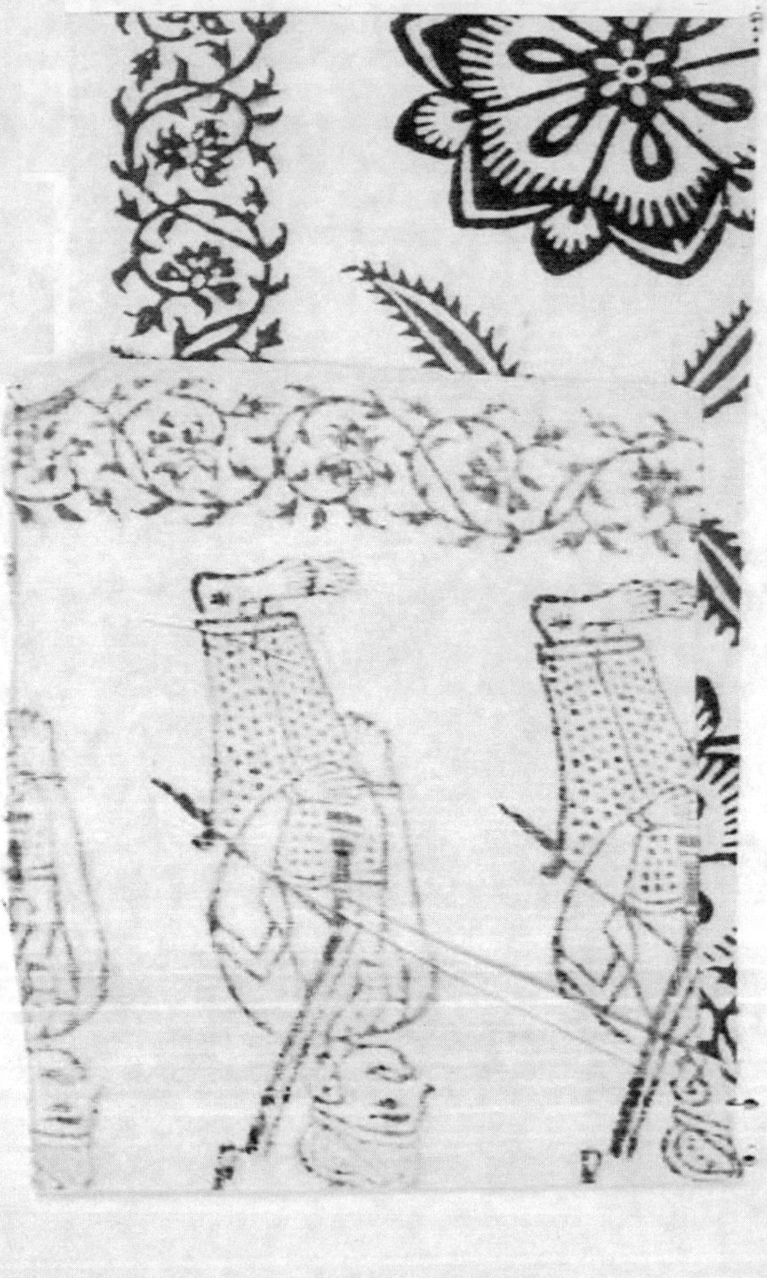

~~Prov. No. 166.~~ No. 478

INDIA FABRICS.

CHINTZES (UNGLAZED).

"Palampore" or bed cover. Cotton; printed border.

SEAM 14 INCHES FROM THE EDGE.

Length 2 yards 14 inches; width 1 yard 14 inches. Weight 13 oz. Price 2s.

From MASULIPATAM; MADRAS.

~~Prov. No. 233.~~ No. 477

INDIA FABRICS.

COTTON.

"Soojney" or counterpane.

Length 2 yards 9 inches; width 1 yard 4 inches. Weight 2 lbs. Price 4s. 6d.

From KURNOOL; MADRAS.

~~Prov. No. 939.~~ No. 480

INDIA FABRICS.

COTTON.

"Soojney" or counterpane.

COLORED THREAD.

Length 2 yards 9 inches; width 1 yard 4 inches. Weight 2 lbs. Price 4s. 6d.

From KURNOOL; MADRAS.

~~Prov. No. 998.~~ No. 481

INDIA FABRICS.

KINCOB.

Silk with gold flowers.

MADE UP INTO ALL KINDS OF GARMENTS FOR BOTH SEXES OF RICHER CLASSES.

Length of piece 5 yards; width 26 inches. Weight of piece 11 oz. Price 2*l.* 16*s.*

From TRICHINOPOLY; MADRAS.

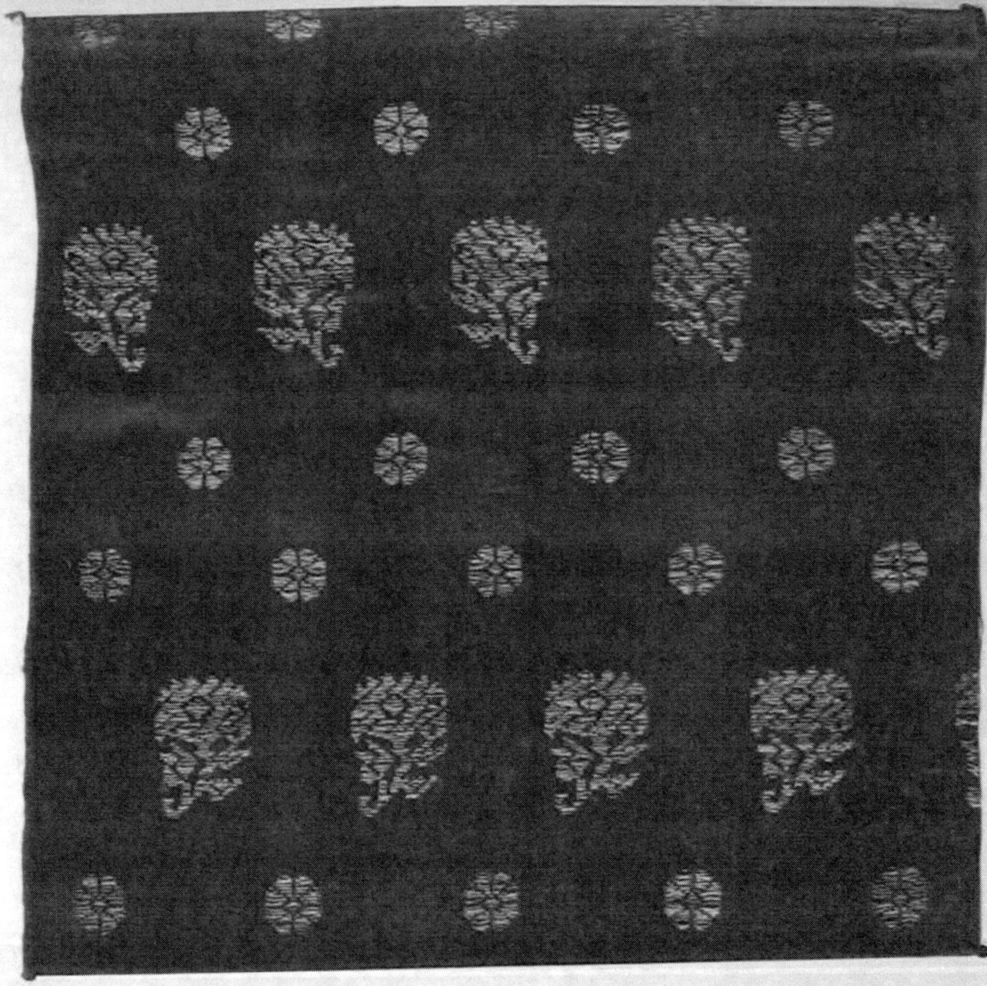

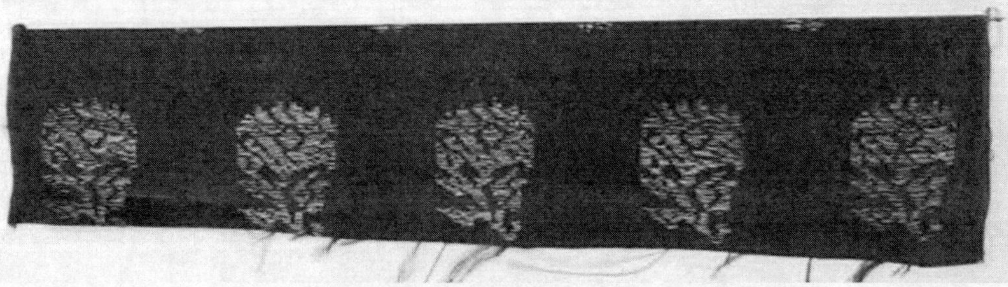

THE TEXTILE MANUFACTURERS OF INDIA

JOHN FORBES WATSON

VOLUME:-13

1866

~~Prov. No. 298.~~ No. 481

INDIA FABRICS.

KINCOB.

Silk with gold flowers.

MADE UP INTO ALL KINDS OF GARMENTS FOR BOTH SEXES OF RICHER CLASSES.

Length of piece 5 yards; width 26 inches. Weight of piece 11 oz. Price 2l. 16s.

From TRICHINOPOLY; MADRAS.

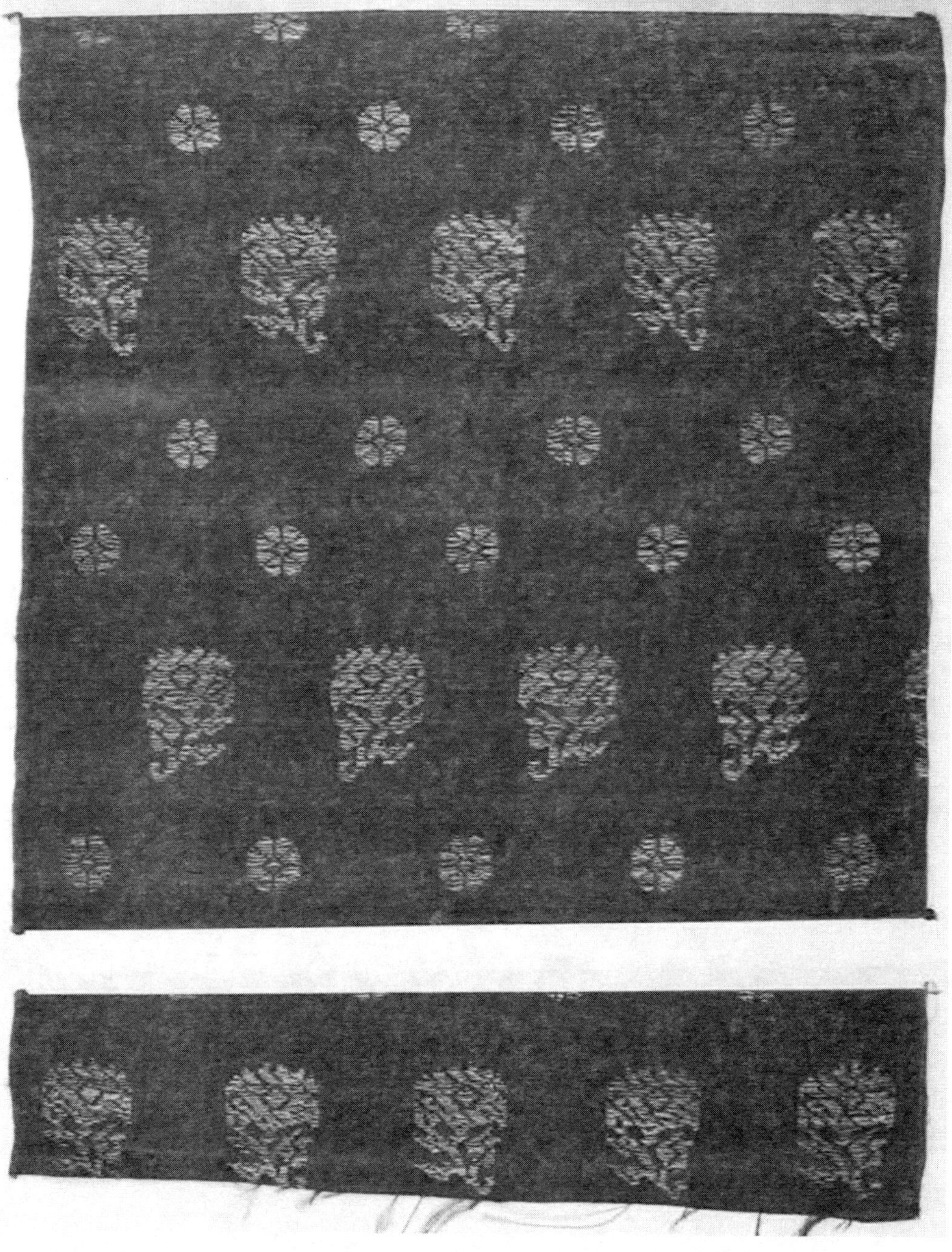

~~Prov. No. 906.~~ No. 482

INDIA FABRICS.

KINCOB.

Satin, with stripes and flowers of gold and silver.

USED FOR GARMENTS OF ALL KINDS AMONGST RICHER CLASSES.

Length 5 yards 9 inches; width 34 inches. Weight 15 oz. Price 1*l*. 11*s*.

From TANJORE; MADRAS.

~~Prov. No. 230.~~ No. 483

INDIA FABRICS.

KINCOB.

Satin, gold flowers.

Length 4 yards 27 inches; width 24 inches. Weight 14 oz. Price 3*l.*

From TRICHINOPOLY; MADRAS.

~~Prov. No. 229.~~ No. 484

INDIA FABRICS.

KINCOB.

Silk, with gold flowers.

USED FOR PETTICOATS.

Length 5 yards; width 27 inches. Weight 11 oz. Price 2*l.* 10*s.*

From TRICHINOPOLY; MADRAS.

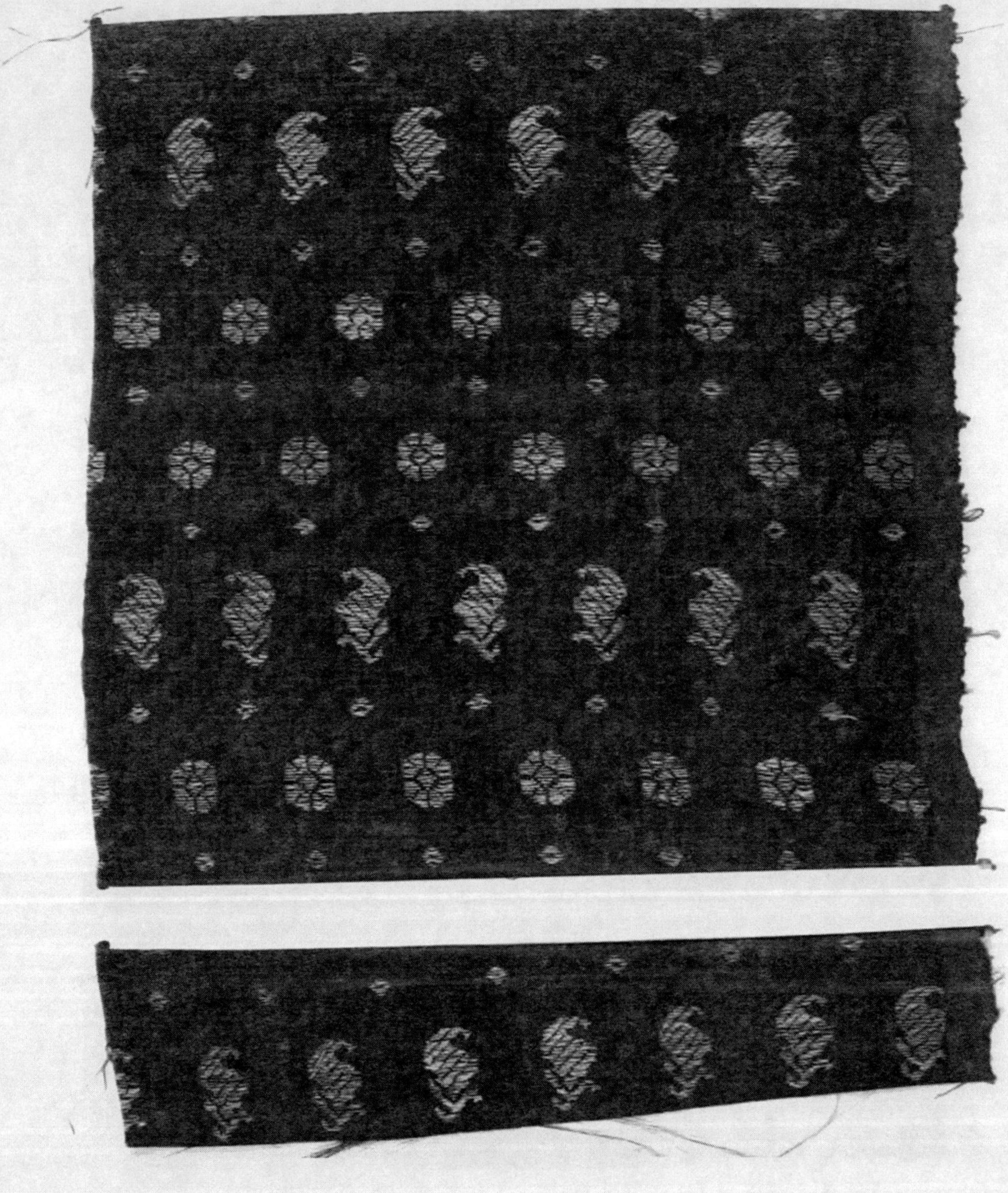

~~Prov. No. [illegible].~~ No. 485

INDIA FABRICS.

SILK BROCADE.

Silk, with flowers of white silk.

Length 5 yards 14 inches, width 31 inches. Weight 1 lb. 8 oz.

From HYDERABAD; DECCAN. *Bought in* MADRAS.

~~Prov. No. 370.~~ No. 484

INDIA FABRICS.

SATIN, "MUSHROO."

Silk surface; cotton back. Flower embroidered in loom.

Length 5 yards 9 inches; width 32 inches. Weight 1 lb. 10½ oz. Price 2*l.*

From HYDERABAD; DECCAN. *Bought in* MADRAS.

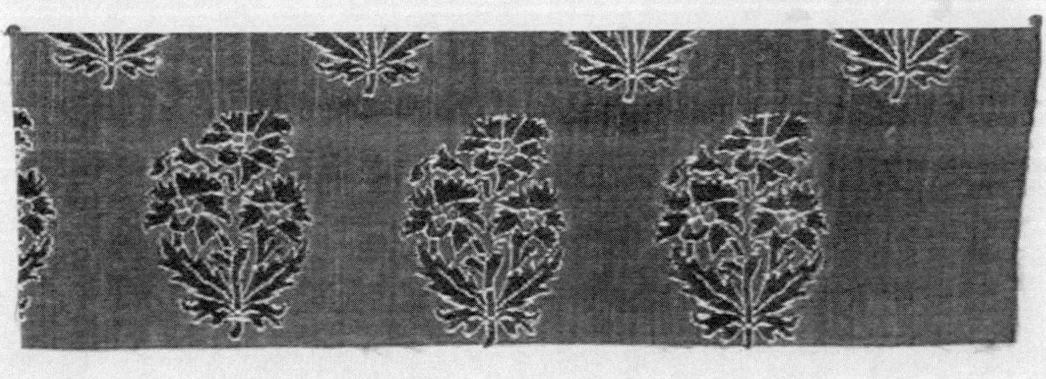

~~Prov. No. 275.~~ No. 481

INDIA FABRICS.

SATIN, "MUSHROO."

Silk surface; cotton back. Loom embroidered flowers.

Length 5 yards; width 30½ inches. Weight 1 lb. 7 oz. Price 2*l.*

From HYDERABAD; DECCAN. *Bought in* MADRAS.

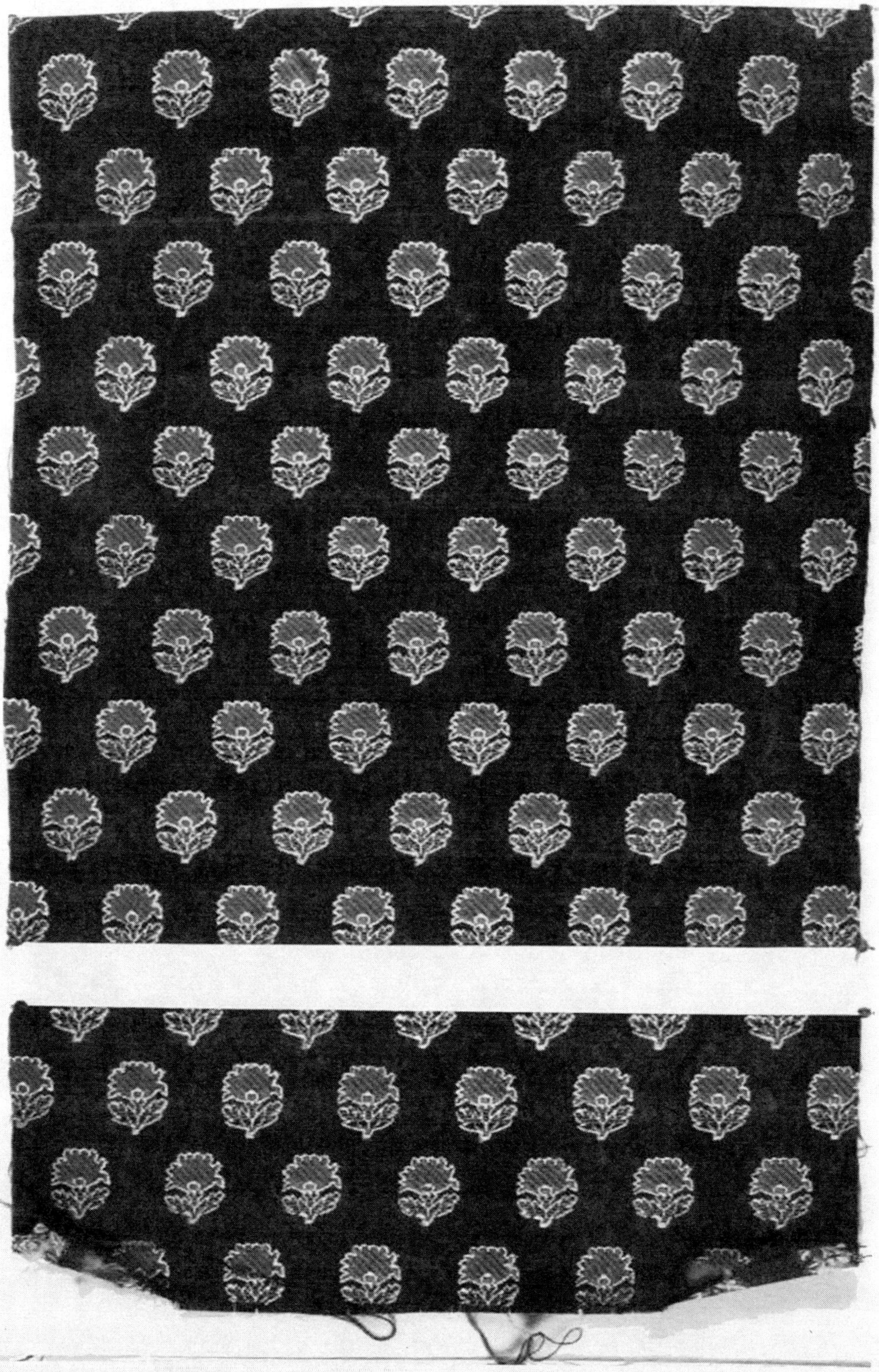

~~Prov. No. 225.~~ No. 488

INDIA FABRICS.

SATIN. "MUSHROO."

Silk surface; cotton back. Flowered with gold and silk.

Length 4 yards 18 inches; width 35 inches. Weight 1 lb. 12 oz. Price 2l. 2s.

From TRICHINOPOLY; MADRAS.

~~Prov. No. 297.~~ No. 489

INDIA FABRICS.

SATIN. "MUSHROO."

Silk surface; cotton back. Flowered in gold, with silk stripes.

Length 4 yards 27 inches; width 24 inches. Weight 14 oz. Price 2*l.* 4*s.*

From TRICHINOPOLY; MADRAS.

~~Prov. No. 372.~~ No. 490

INDIA FABRICS.

SATIN, "MUSHROO."

Silk surface; cotton back. Gold stripes.

Length 6 yards; width 28 inches. Weight 1 lb. 5 oz.

From HYDERABAD; DECCAN.

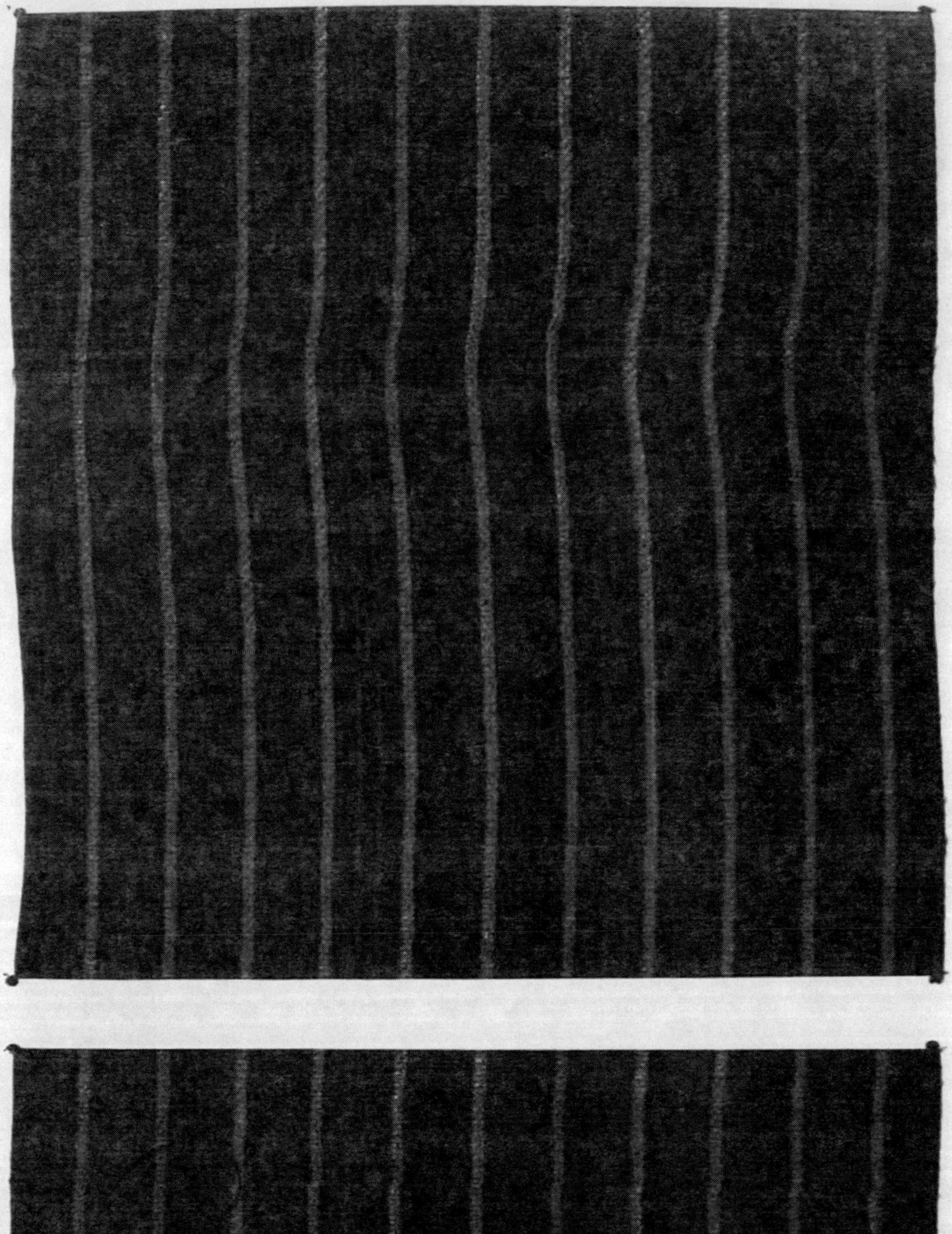

~~Prov. No. 224.~~ No. 491

INDIA FABRICS.

SATIN, "MUSHROO."

Silk surface: cotton back. Dotted with gold. Striped.

Length 4 yards 18 inches; width 24 inches. Weight 14 oz. Price 2*l.* 4*s.*

From TANJORE; MADRAS.

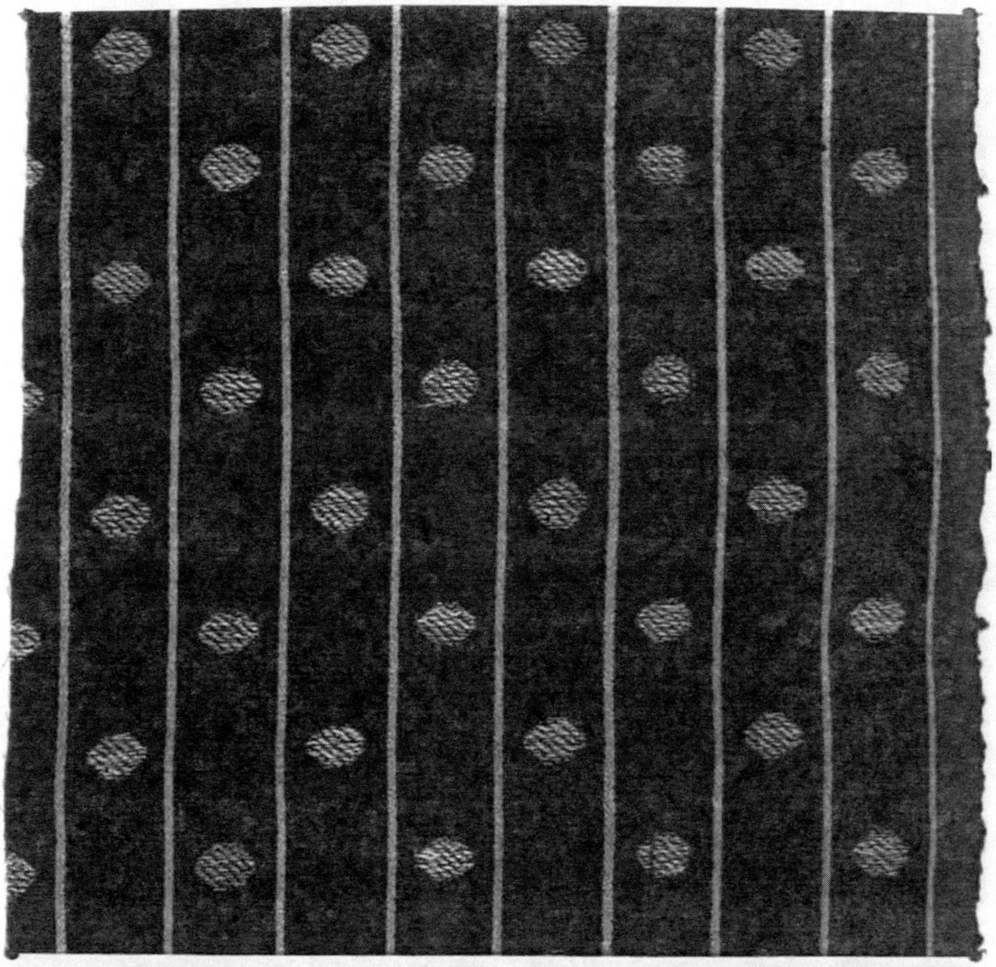

~~Prov. No. 211.~~ No. 492

INDIA FABRICS.

SATIN. "MUSHROO."

Silk flowered surface; cotton back.

Length 4 yards 24 inches; width 29 inches. Weight 11 oz. Price 11s. 6d.

From TANJORE; MADRAS.

~~Prov. No. 369.~~ No. 493

INDIA FABRICS.

SATIN. "MUSHROO."

Silk surface; cotton back. Colored stripes and spots.

Length 6 yards 15 inches; width 1 yard. Weight 1 lb. 10¾ oz. Price 16s.

From TANJORE; MADRAS.

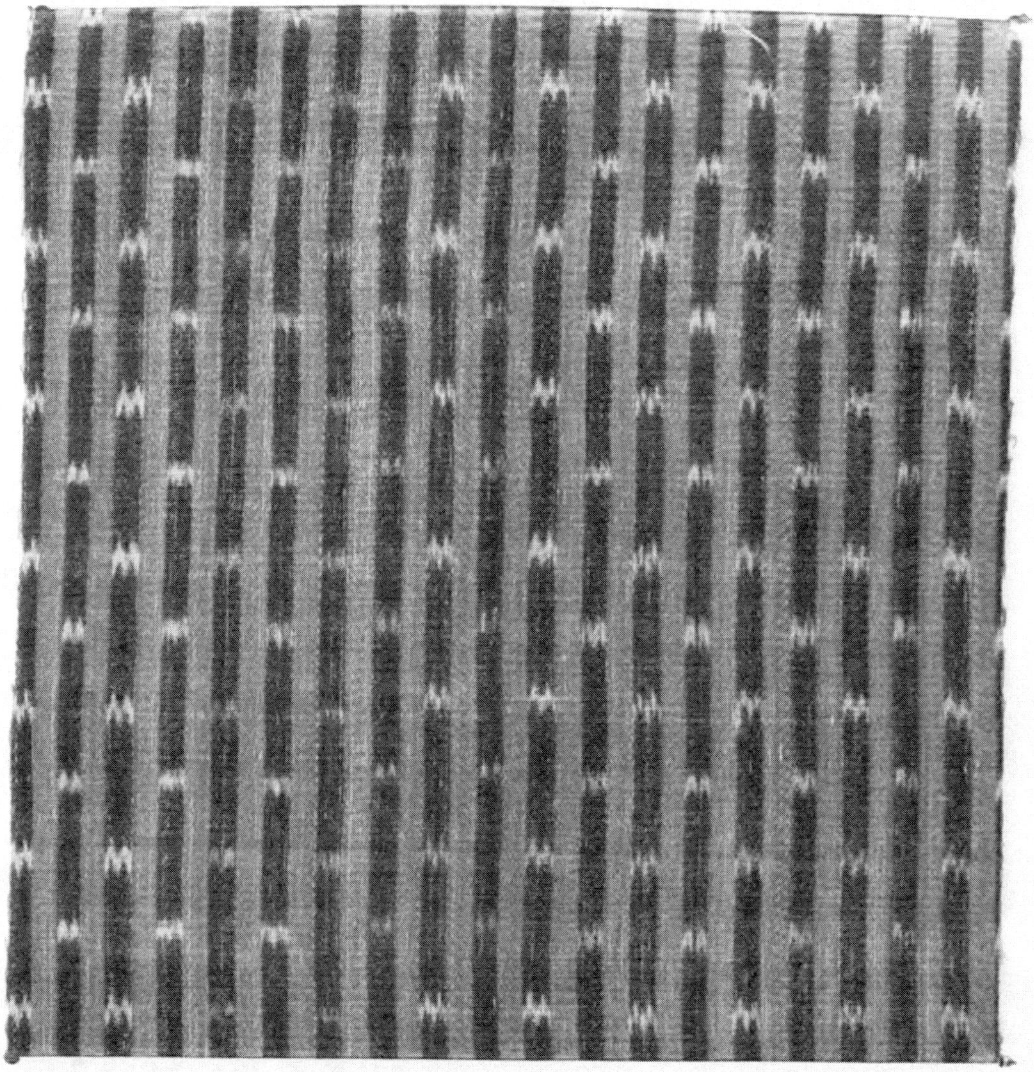

~~Prov. No. 366.~~ No. 494

INDIA FABRICS.

SATIN, "MUSHROO."

Silk surface; cotton back. Flowered stripes.

Length 6 yards 30 inches; width 1 yard. Weight 1 lb. 2 oz. Price 1*l.* 16*s.*

From HYDERABAD; DECCAN. *Bought in* MADRAS.

~~Prov. No. 991.~~ No. 495

INDIA FABRICS.

SATIN, "MUSHROO."

Silk surface; cotton back.

Length 6 yards 9 inches; width 33 inches. Weight 1 lb. 7 oz. Price 16s.

From TANJORE; MADRAS.

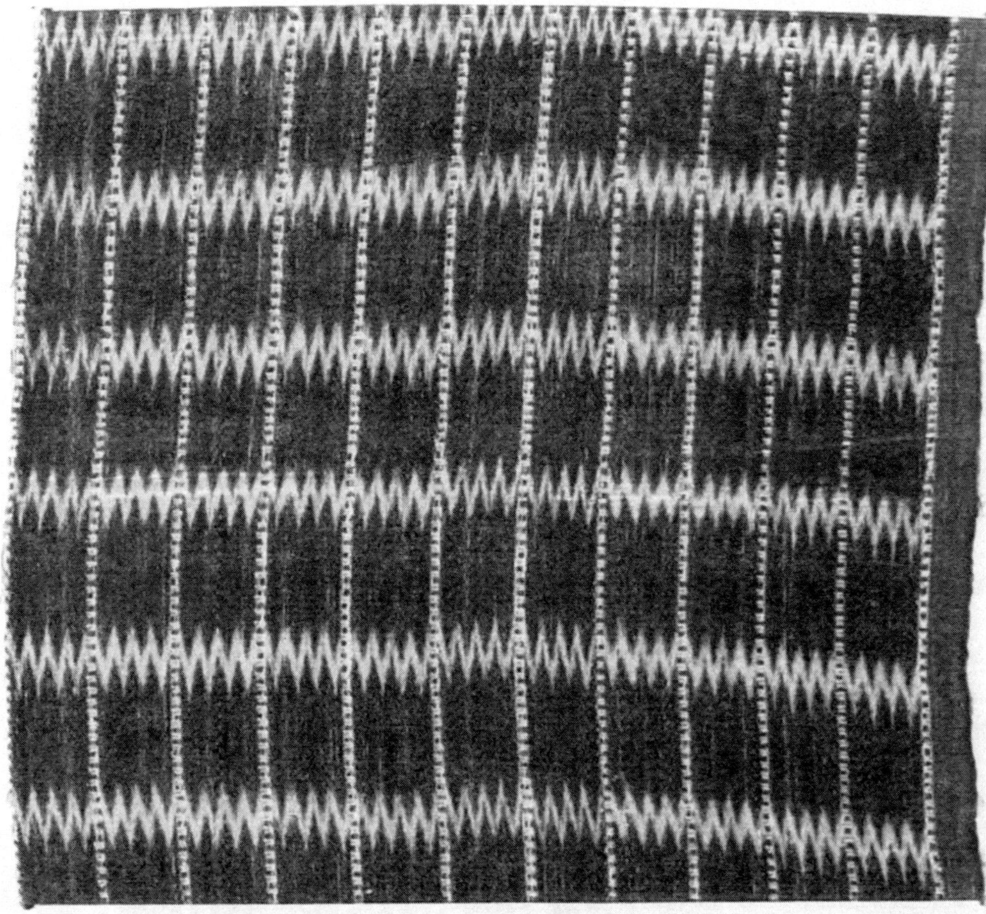

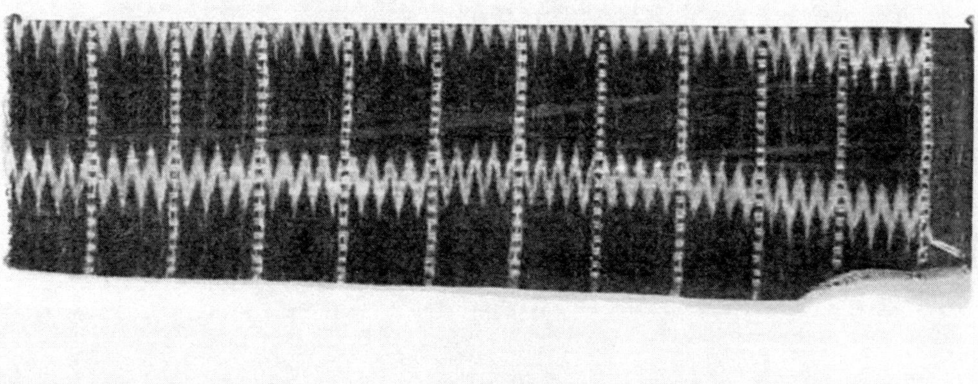

~~Prov. No. 220.~~ No. 496

INDIA FABRICS.

SATIN, "MUSHROO."

Silk surface; cotton back. Colored stripes and flowers.

Length 5 yards; width 1 yard. Weight 1 lb. 10 oz. Price 17s.

From TRICHINOPOLY; MADRAS.

~~Prov. No. 364.~~ No. 497

INDIA FABRICS.

SATIN. "MUSHROO."

Silk surface; cotton back.

PATTERN OF VERY FREQUENT OCCURRENCE.

Length 6 yards; width 31 inches. Weight 1 lb. 4½ oz. Price 1*l*. 7*s*.

From HYDERABAD; DECCAN.

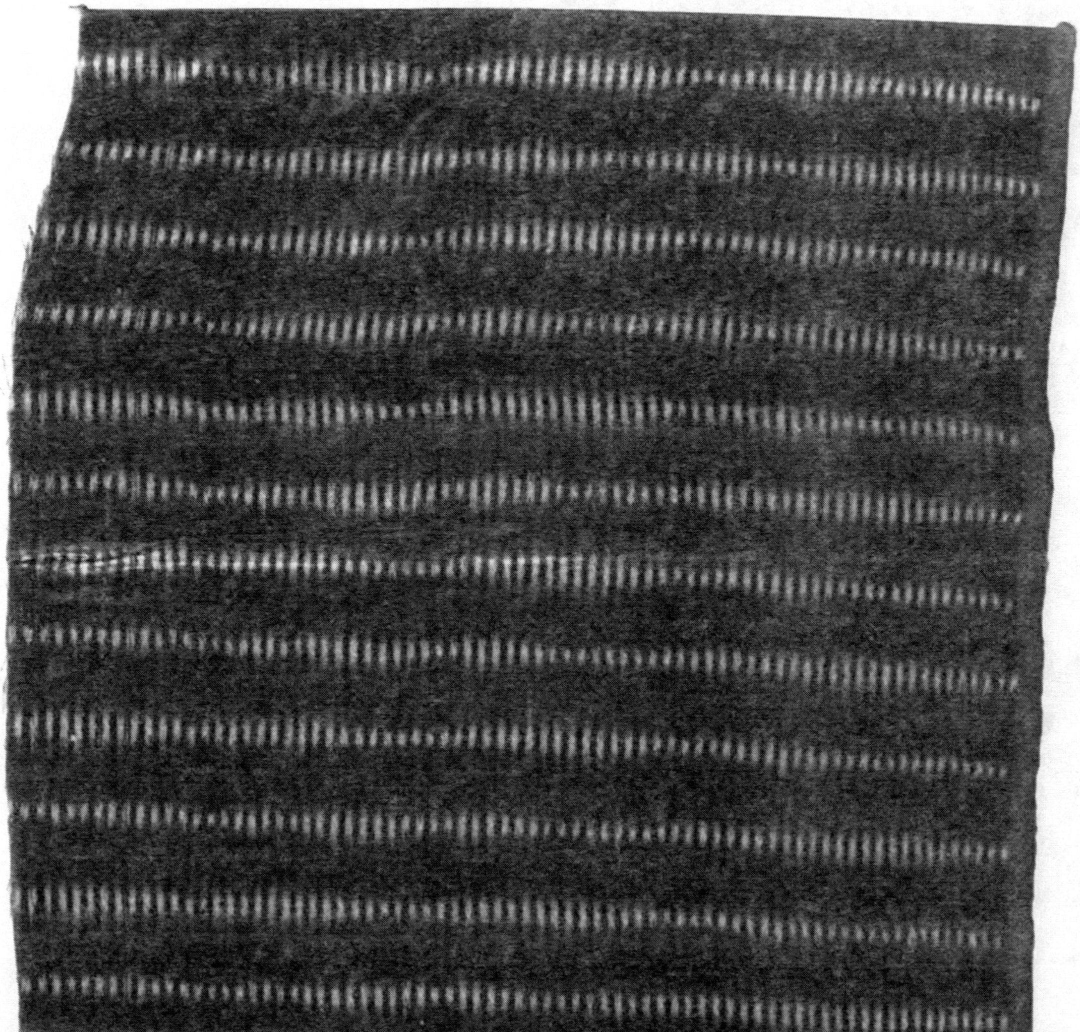

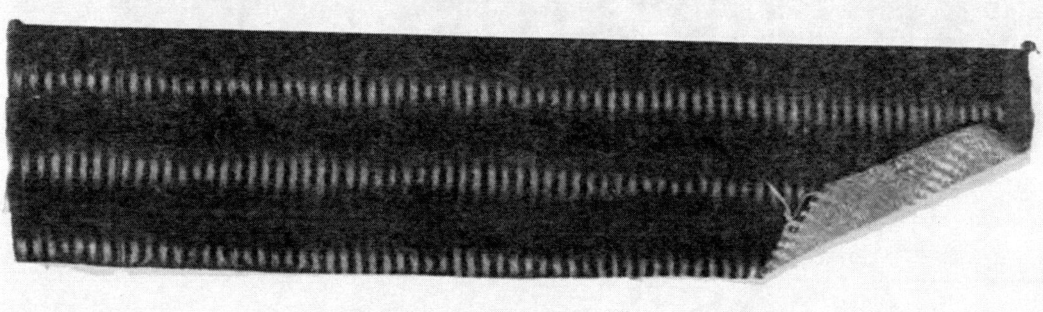

~~Prev. No. 217.~~ No. 498

INDIA FABRICS.

SATIN, "MUSHROO."

Silk surface; cotton back. Parti-colored stripes.

Length 5 yards; width 1 yard. Weight 1 lb. 5 oz. Price 17s.

From TRICHINOPOLY; MADRAS.

~~Prev. No. 867.~~ No. 477

INDIA FABRICS.

SATIN, "MUSHROO."

Silk surface; cotton back. Flowered stripes.

Length 5 yards 32 inches; width 30½ inches. Weight 1 lb. 4 oz. Price 1*l.* 18*s.*

From HYDERABAD; DECCAN.

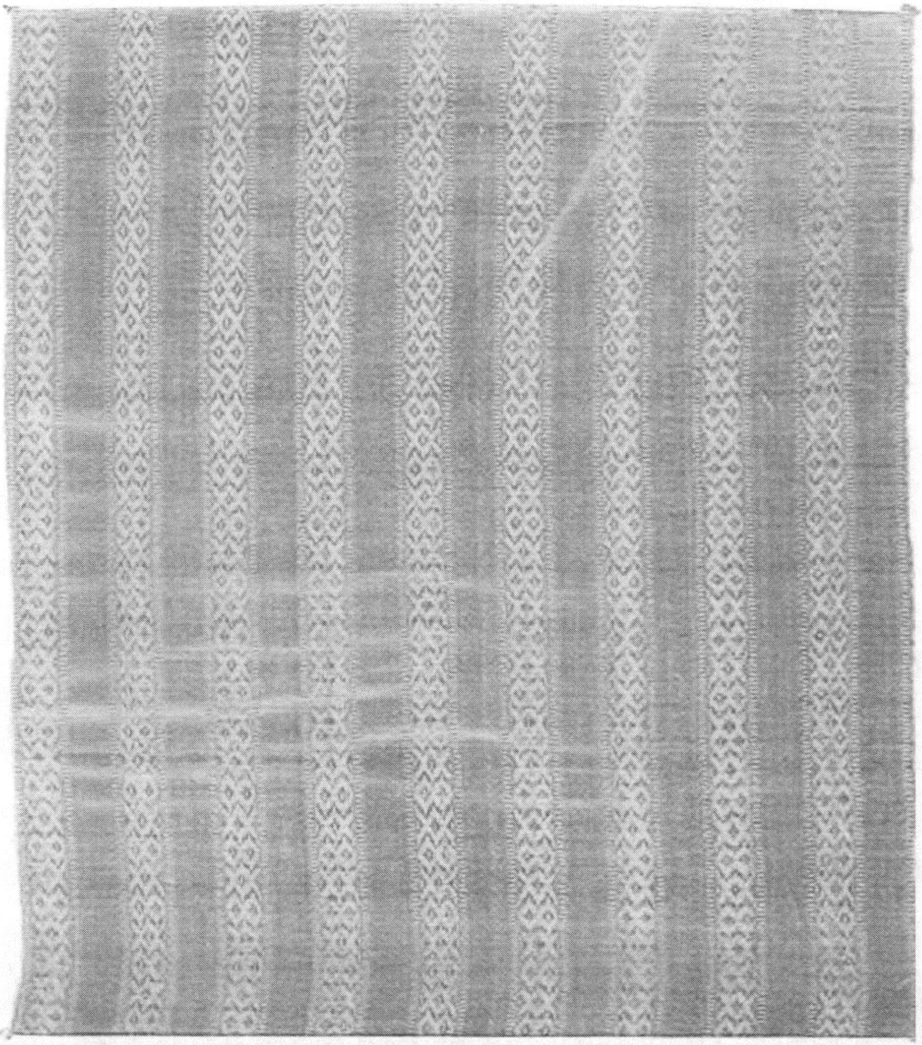

~~Prov. No. 365.~~ No. 506

INDIA FABRICS.

SATIN, "MUSHROO."

Silk surface; cotton back. Plain Pink.

Length 5 yards 31 inches; width 31 inches. Weight 1 lb. 2 oz. Price 1*l.* 18*s.*

From HYDERABAD; DECCAN.

~~Prov. No. 378.~~ No. 501

INDIA FABRICS.

SATIN, "MUSHROO."

Silk surface; cotton back.

FAVORITE PATTERN BOTH AT THE UNDERMENTIONED PLACE AND AT BENARES.

Length 6 yards; width 32 inches. Weight 1 lb. 3½ oz. Price 1*l.* 16*s.*

From HYDERABAD; DECCAN. *Bought in* MADRAS.

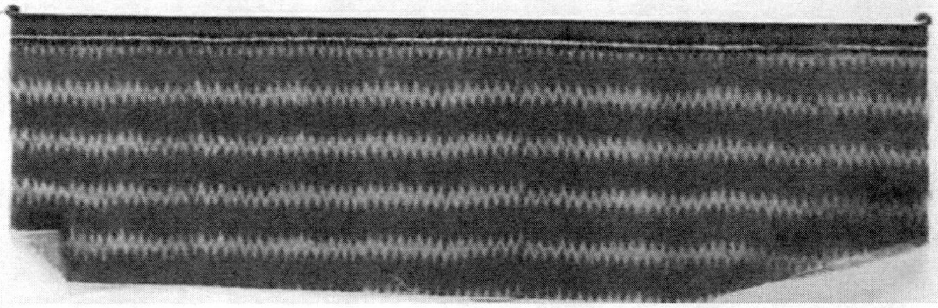

~~Prov. No. 363.~~ No. 502

INDIA FABRICS.

SATIN, "MUSHROO."

Silk surface; cotton back. Plain purple.

Length 3 yards 20 inches; width 34 inches. Weight 13 oz. Price 11s.

From TRICHINOPOLY; MADRAS.

~~Prov. No. 222.~~ No. 503

INDIA FABRICS.

SATIN, "MUSHROO."

Silk surface; cotton back. Crimson and white irregular stripes.

FAVORITE PATTERN.

Length 6 yards 9 inches; width 33 inches. Weight 1 lb. 9 oz. Price 17s.

From TRICHINOPOLY; MADRAS.

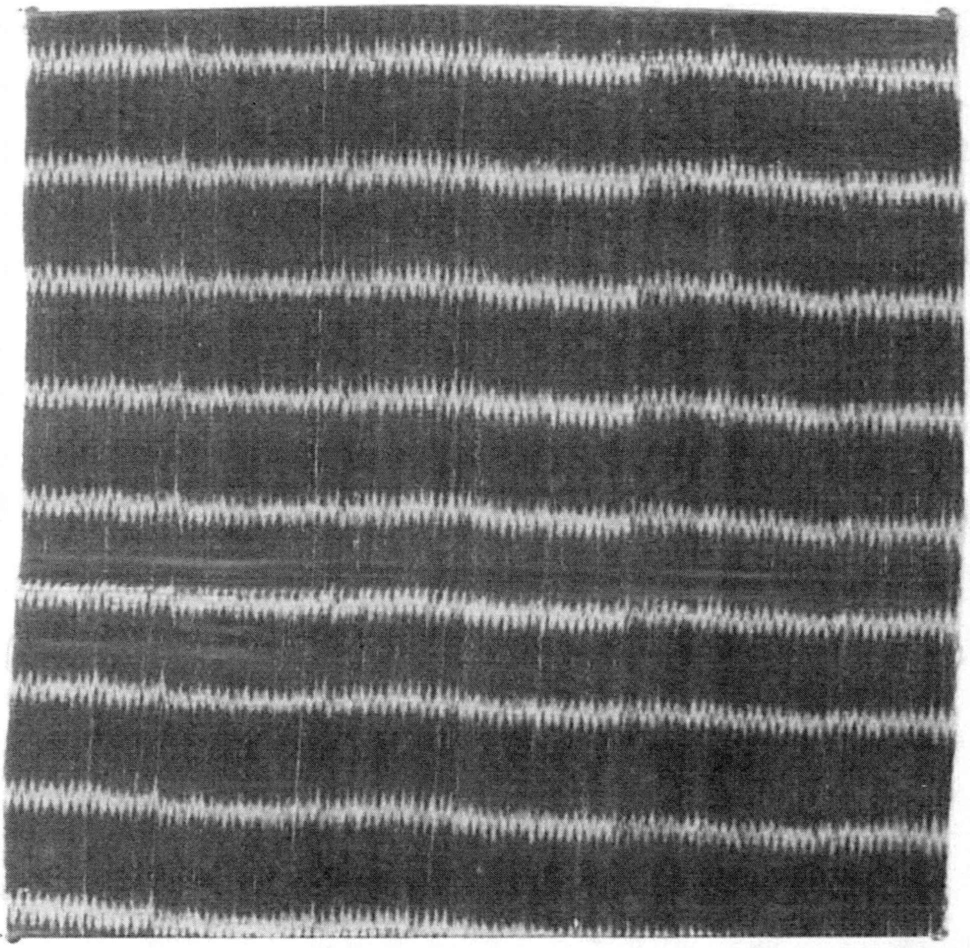

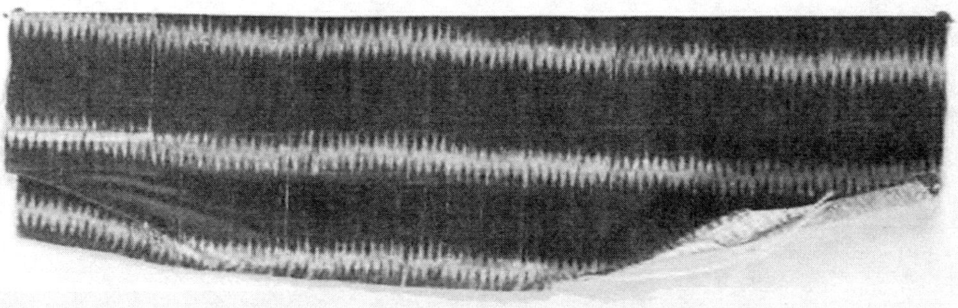

~~Prov. No. 261.~~ No. 504

INDIA FABRICS.

SATIN, "MUSHROO."

Silk surface; cotton back.

A FAVORITE PATTERN.

Length 5 yards 31 inches; width 26 inches. Weight 1 lb. 2 oz. Price 1*l.* 18*s.*

From HYDERABAD; DECCAN.

~~Prov. No. 859.~~ No. 503

INDIA FABRICS.

SATIN. "MUSHROO."

Silk surface; cotton back.

WORN IN VARIETY OF COLORS.

Length 6 yards 14 inches; width 34½ inches. Weight 1 lb. 11½ oz. Price 1*l.*

From TANJORE; MADRAS.

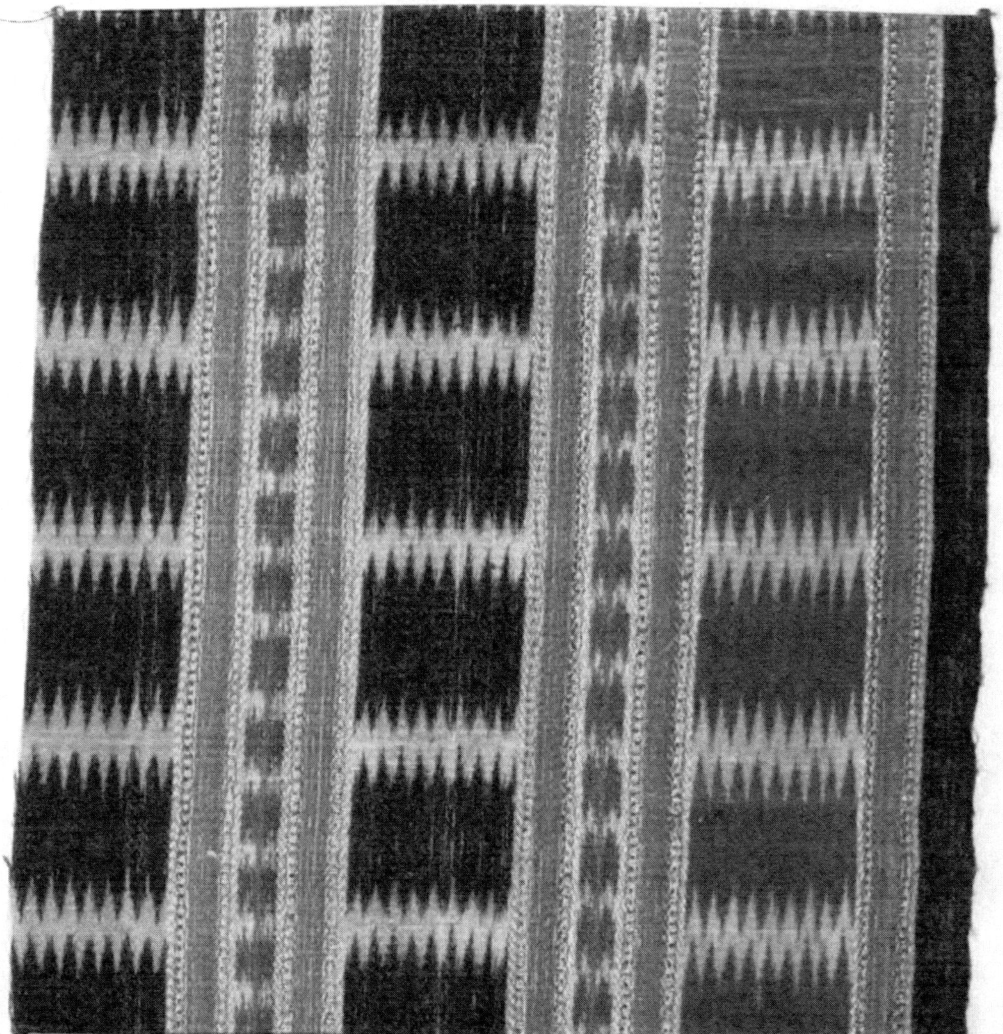

~~Prov. No. 993.~~ No. 504

INDIA FABRICS.

SATIN. "MUSHROO."

Silk surface; cotton back. Puce color. Wavy stripes.

FAVORITE PATTERN.

Length 4 yards 27 inches ; width 35 inches. Weight 1 lb. 6 oz. Price 17s.

From TRICHINOPOLY ; MADRAS.

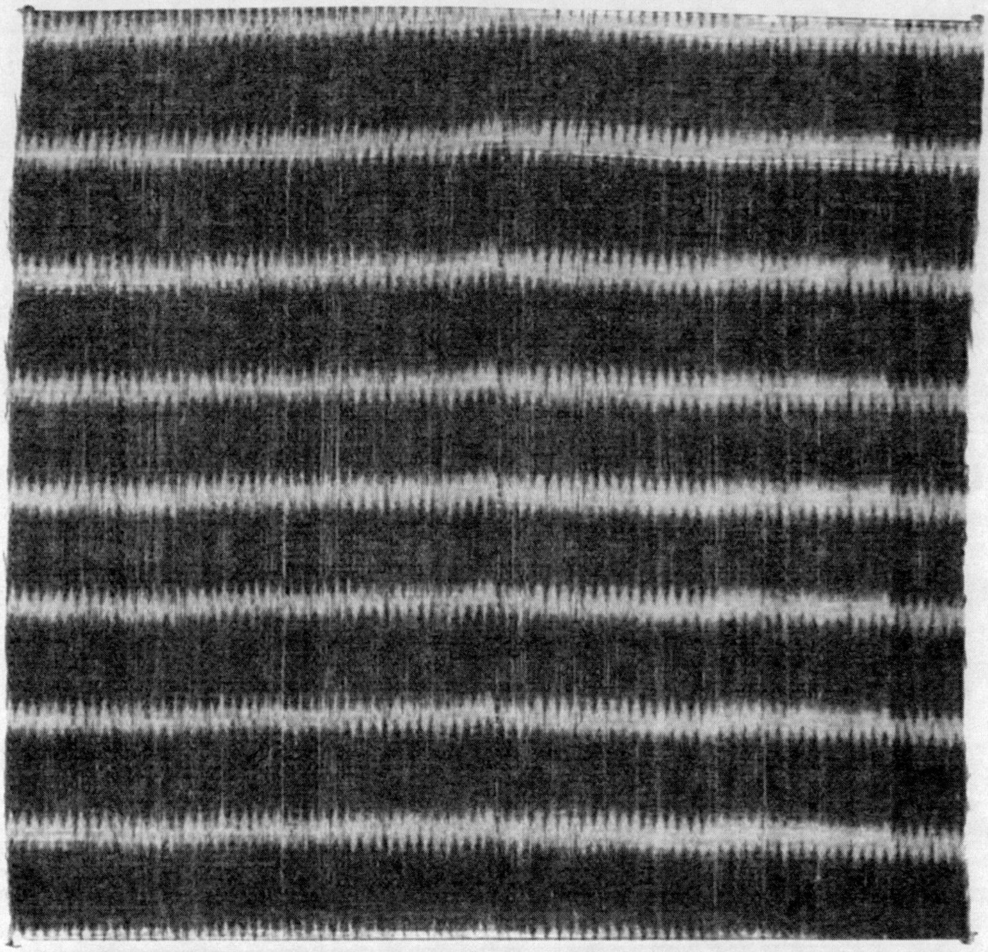

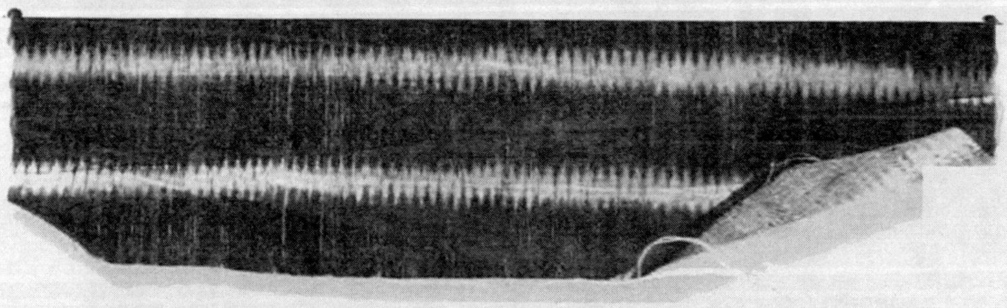

~~Previous No. 376.~~ No. 501

INDIA FABRICS.

SATIN. "MUSHROO."

Silk surface: cotton back. Plain green color.

Length 5 yards 37 inches; width 30½ inches. Weight 1 lb. 2½ oz. Price 1l. 18s.

From HYDERABAD; DECCAN.

~~Prov. No. 210.~~ No. 508

INDIA FABRICS.

SATIN. "MUSHROO."

Silk surface; cotton back. Crimson, with narrow white stripes.

Length 5 yards; width 1 yard. Weight 1 lb. 5 oz. Price 17*s*.

From TRICHINOPOLY; MADRAS.

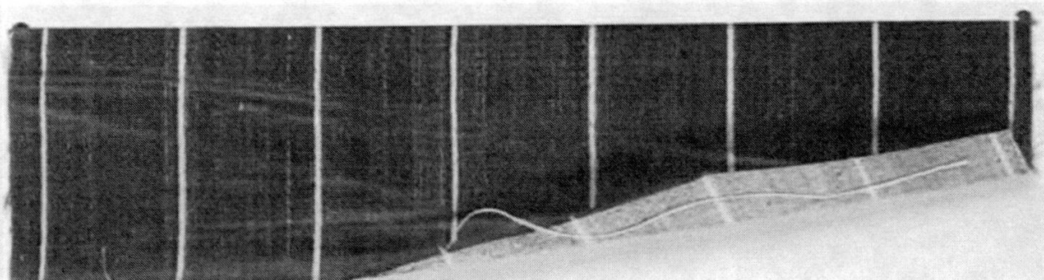

~~Prov. No. 916.~~

No. 509

INDIA FABRICS.

SATIN. "MUSHROO."

Silk surface; cotton back. Orange, with white stripes.

Length 6 yards 15 inches; width 1 yard. Weight 2 lbs. 7 oz. Price 18s.

From TANJORE; MADRAS.

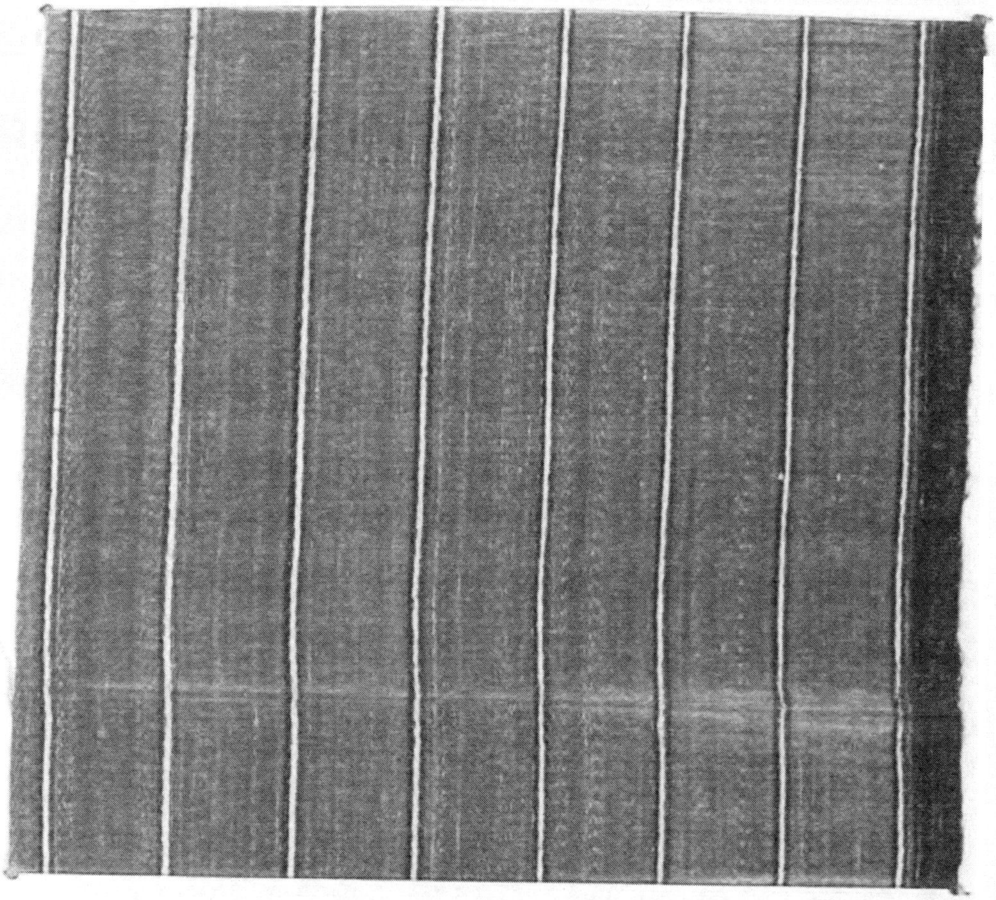

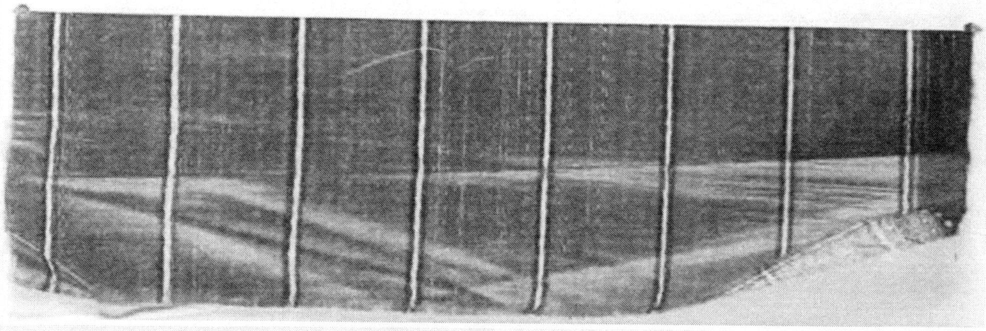

~~Prov. No. 360.~~ No. 510

INDIA FABRICS.

SATIN. "MUSHROO."

Silk surface; cotton back. Plain crimson.

Length 6 yards; width 32 inches. Weight 1 lb. 4 oz. Price 1*l.* 16*s.*

From HYDERABAD; DECCAN.

~~Prov. No. 371~~.

No. 571

INDIA FABRICS.

SATIN. "MUSHROO."

Silk surface : cotton back. Bright yellow, with colored stripes.

Length 5 yards 27 inches ; width 27 inches. Weight 1 lb. 6 oz. Price of each 1*l*. 16*s*.

From HYDERABAD ; DECCAN.

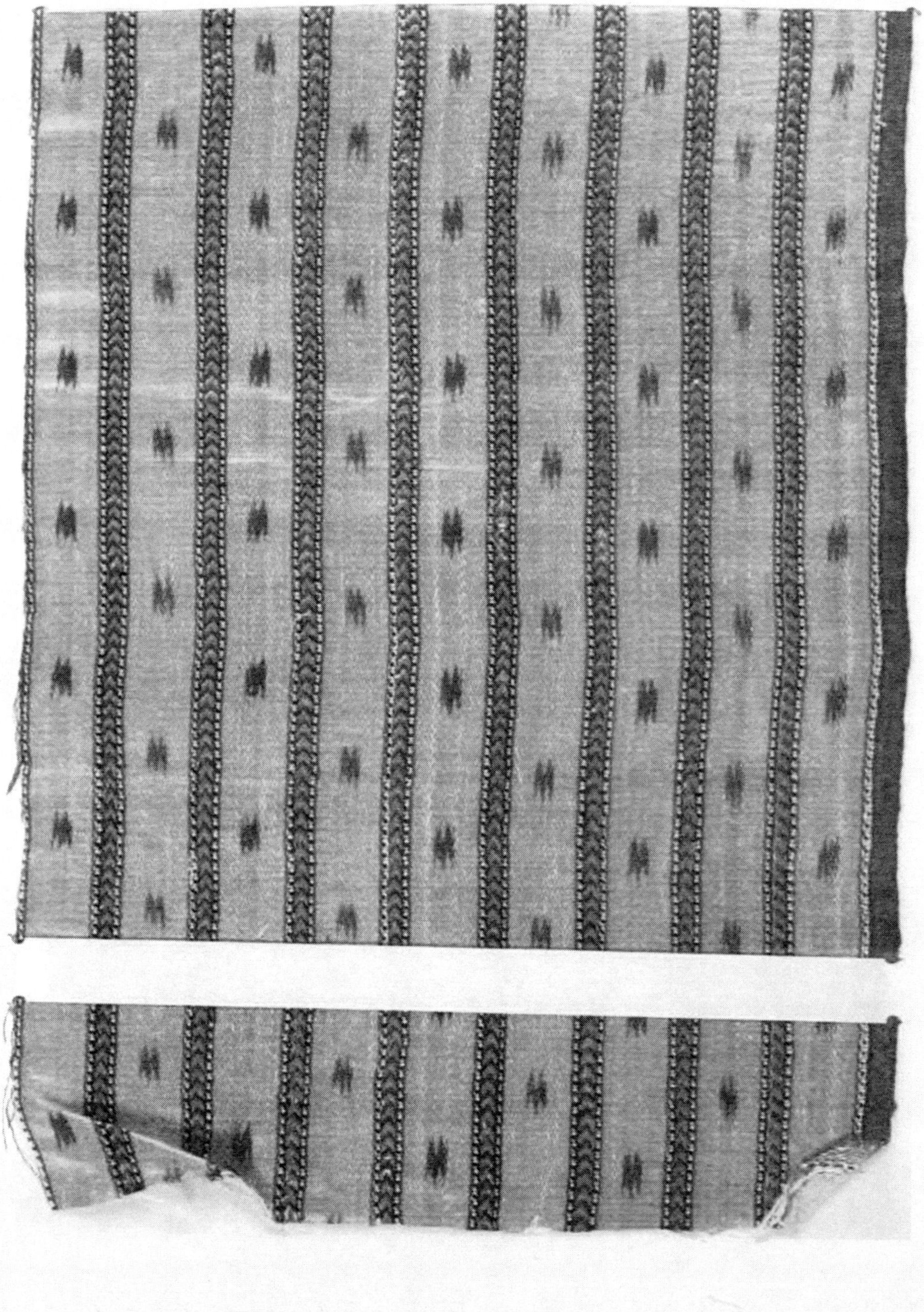

~~Prov. No. 374.~~ No. 517

INDIA FABRICS.

SATIN. "MUSHROO."

Silk surface; cotton back. Pink flowered stripes.

Length 5 yards 33 inches; width 30 inches. Weight 1 lb. 1 oz. Price 1*l.* 15*s.*

From HYDERABAD; DECCAN. *Bought in* MADRAS.

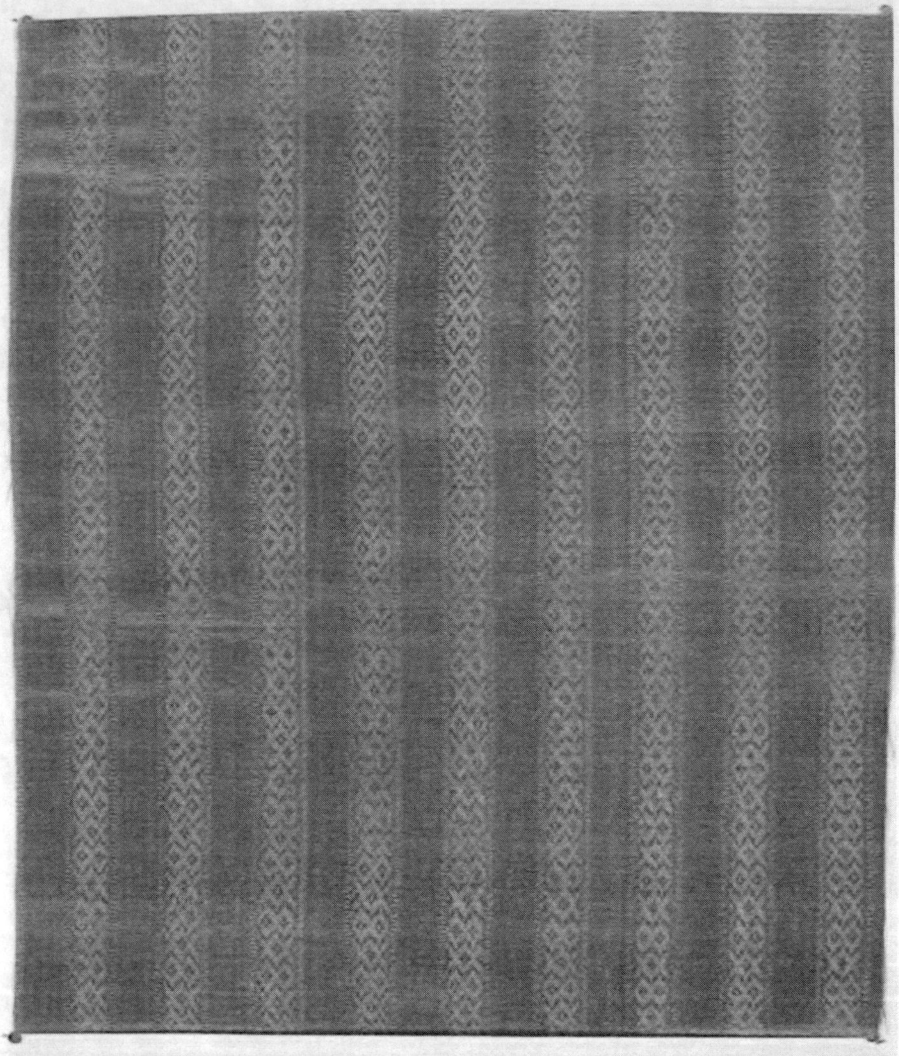

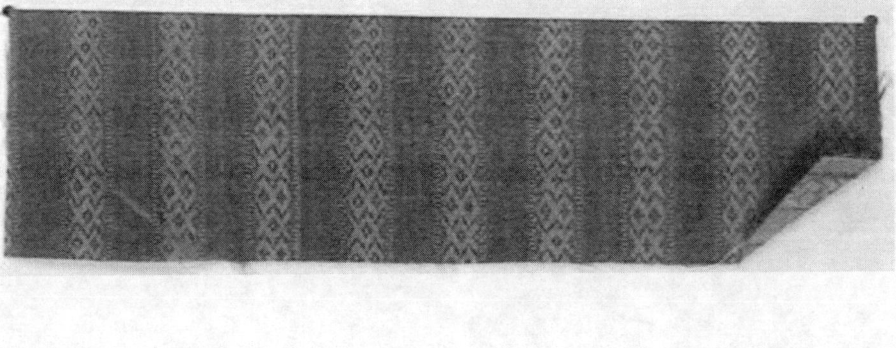

~~Prov. No. 218.~~

No. 513

INDIA FABRICS.

SATIN. "MUSHROO."

Silk surface: cotton back. Broad stripes in colors.

Length 6 yards 14 inches; width 1 yard. Weight 1 lb. 6 oz. Price 14s.

From TRICHINOPOLY; MADRAS.

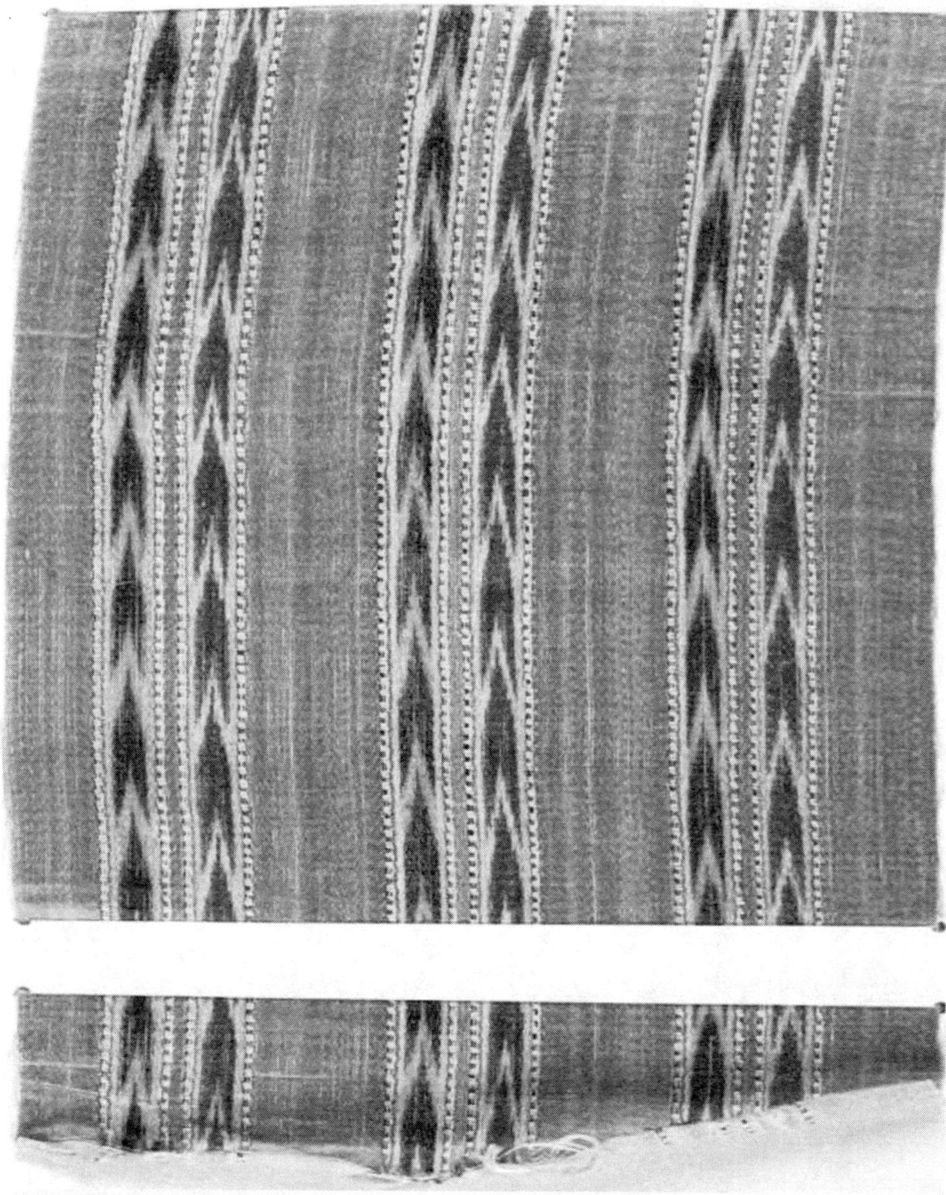

~~Prov. No. 362.~~ No. 574

INDIA FABRICS.

SATIN, "MUSHROO."

Silk surface; cotton back. Plain red.

Length 4 yards 22 inches; width 31 inches. Weight 10½ oz. Price 1*l.* 18*s.*

From HYDERABAD; DECCAN. *Bought in* MADRAS.

~~Prov. No. 877.~~ No. 515

INDIA FABRICS.

SATIN. "MUSHROO."

Silk surface; cotton back. Plain white.

Length 4 yards 16 inches; width 32½ inches. Weight 15 oz. Price 1*l.* 9*s.*

From HYDERABAD; DECCAN.

~~Prov. No. 378.~~ No. 574

INDIA FABRICS.

SILK.

Striped silk fabric.

THIN LIGHT MATERIAL USED FOR TROUSERINGS.

Length 9 yards 4 inches ; width 37 inches. Weight 14 oz. Price 1*l*. 10*s*.

From TRICHINOPOLY ; MADRAS.

No. 571

INDIA FABRICS.

SILK.

Silk fabric with flowered stripes.

USED FOR TROUSERINGS.

Length 8 yards 27 inches; width 35 inches. Weight 1 lb. 2 oz. Price 2l. 2s.

From TRICHINOPOLY; MADRAS.

~~Prev. No. 800.~~ No. 518

INDIA FABRICS.

SILK.

Gauze-like fabric.

USED FOR BODICES, PETTICOATS, AND TROUSERINGS.

Length 11 yards; width 33 inches. Weight 14½ oz. Price 2*l*.

From TRICHINOPOLY; MADRAS.

~~Prov. No. 209.~~ No. 519

INDIA FABRICS.

SILK PIECE FOR GARMENTS.

Silk gauze-like fabric.

FOR TROWSERING AND UNDERGARMENTS.

Length 9 yards ; width 34 inches. Weight 12 oz. Price 17s.

From TRICHINOPOLY ; MADRAS.

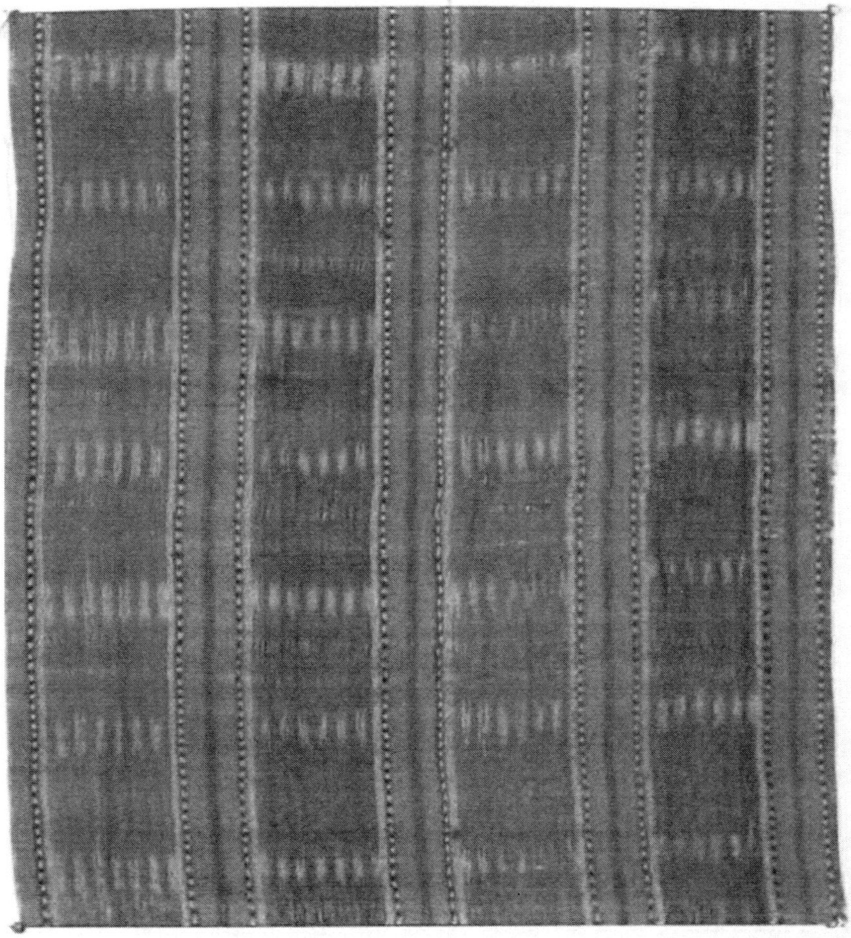

~~Prov. No. 279.~~ No. 520

INDIA FABRICS.

SILK PIECES FOR GARMENTS.

Silk gauze.

USED FOR TROUSERING.

Length 9 yards 6 inches; width 34 inches. Weight $11\frac{1}{2}$ oz. Price 19s.

From TANJORE; MADRAS.

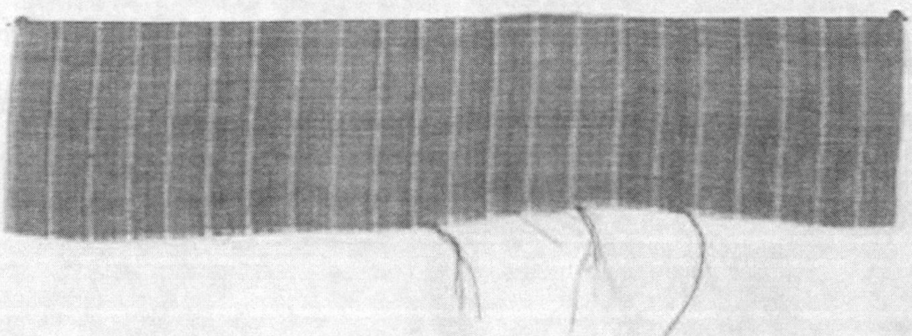

THE TEXTILE MANUFACTURERS OF INDIA

JOHN FORBES WATSON

VOLUME:-14

1866

~~Prov. No. 535.~~ No. 521

INDIA FABRICS.

SILK PIECE GOODS.

Plain red silk.

Extensively used in the Punjab for making up, and also as lining of various kinds of garments.

Length 17 yards 15 inches; width 21¼ inches. Weight 2 lbs. 9¾ oz. Price 3*l.*

From LAHORE.

~~Prov. No. 532.~~ No. 522

INDIA FABRICS.

SILK PIECE GOODS.

Plain fabric.

Length 13 yards 9 inches; width $21\frac{1}{2}$ inches. Weight 1 lb. $8\frac{1}{2}$ oz. Price 1*l.* 16*s.*

From LAHORE; PUNJAB.

~~Prov. No. 528.~~

No. 523

INDIA FABRICS.

SILK PIECE GOODS.

Light green silk (plain).

Length 15 yards 31 inches ; width 20½ inches. Weight 2 lbs. 1 oz. Price 3l.

From LAHORE.

~~Prov. No. 555.~~ No. 524

INDIA FABRICS.

SILK PIECE GOODS.

Silk (shot) piece for dresses.

Length 24 yards; width 20½ inches. Weight 2 lbs. 8¼ oz. Price 3*l.* 9*s.*

From LAHORE.

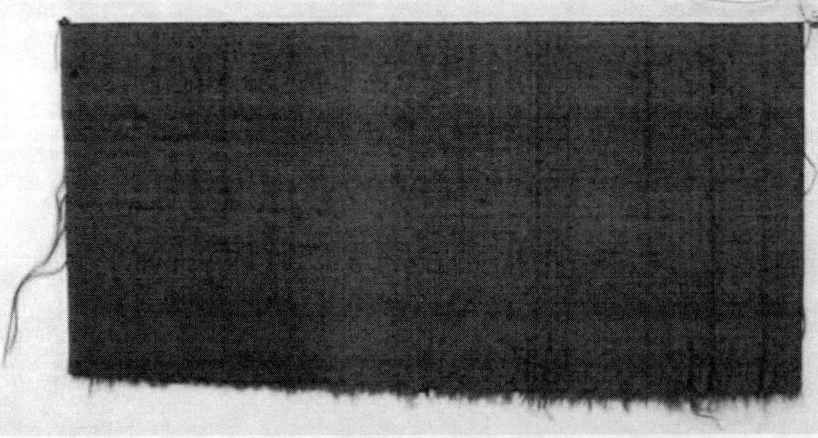

~~Page No. [illegible]~~.

No. 525

INDIA FABRICS.

SILK PIECE GOODS.

Crimson silk with small green stripes.

Length 17 yards 33 inches; width 21½ inches. Weight 2 lbs. 7 oz. Price 3*l.*

From LAHORE.

~~Prov. No. 331~~. No. 526

INDIA FABRICS.

SILK PIECE GOODS.

Silk (yellow) with red stripes.

Length 15 yards ; width 22 inches. Weight 2 lbs. 3 oz. Price 4*l.* 6*s.*

From LAHORE.

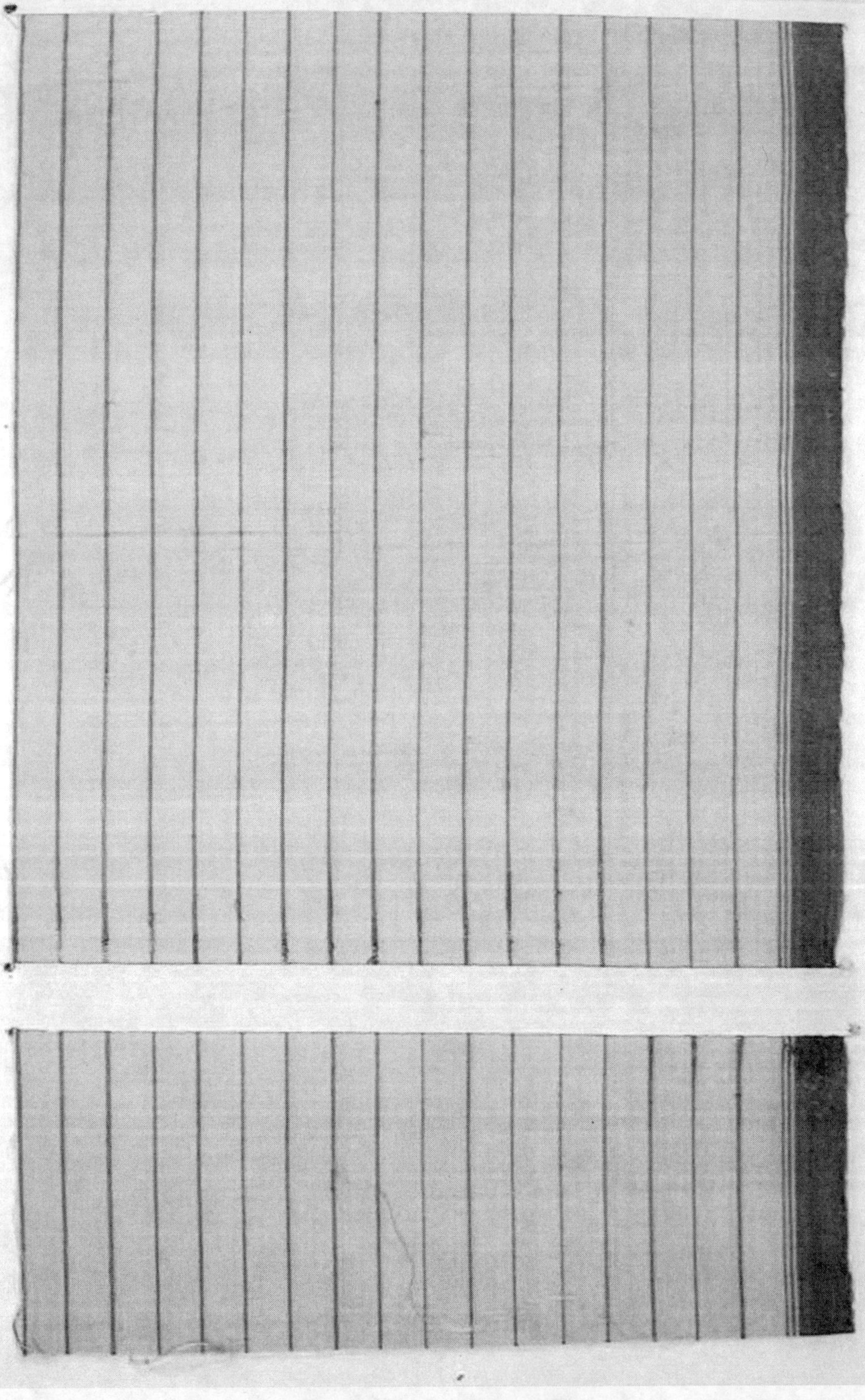

~~Prov. No. 552~~.

No. 52

INDIA FABRICS.

SILK PIECE GOODS.

Crimson silk with white stripes.

Length 18 yards; width 21½ inches. Weight 2 lbs. 8 oz. Price 3l. 6s.

From LAHORE.

~~Prov. No. 607.~~ No. 528

INDIA FABRICS.

SILK PIECE GOODS.

Green silk with red stripes.

Length 16 yards 15 inches; width 21 inches. Weight 2 lbs. 2¼ oz. Price 3*l.*

From LAHORE.

~~[illegible]~~ No. 527

INDIA FABRICS.

SILK PIECE GOODS.

Crimson silk with yellow stripes.

Length 15 yards 26 inches; width 21½ inches. Weight 2 lbs. 5 oz. Price 2*l.* 16*s.*

From LAHORE.

~~Prov. No. 686.~~ No. 530

INDIA FABRICS.

SILK PIECE GOODS.

Puce silk with red stripes.

Length 16 yards 18 inches : width 21 inches. Weight 1 lb. 13¼ oz. Price 2l. 6s.

From LAHORE.

~~Prev. No. 606.~~ No. 531

INDIA FABRICS.

SILK PIECE GOODS.

Purple silk with yellow stripes.

Length 8 yards; width 19 inches. Weight 10¾ oz. Price 1*l.* 2*s.* 6*d.*

From DERA ISHMAEL KHAN.

~~[illegible]~~. No. 532

INDIA FABRICS.

SILK PIECE GOODS.

Red silk (Golabee Durreeaee).

Length 6 yards 11 inches; width 12 inches. Weight 4 oz. Price 10s. 6d.

From AGRA; BENGAL.

~~Prov. No. 554.~~ No. 533

INDIA FABRICS.

SILK PIECE GOODS.

"Sungee Charkhanah" check silk.

Length 4 yards 33 inches; width 27 inches. Weight $7\frac{3}{4}$ oz. Price 1*l.* 10*s.*

From BENARES.

~~Prov. No. 560.~~ No. 534

INDIA FABRICS.

SILK PIECE GOODS.

Flowered silk.

Length 5 yards 32 inches; width 28½ inches. Weight 15¾ oz.

From BHAWULPORE; PUNJAB.

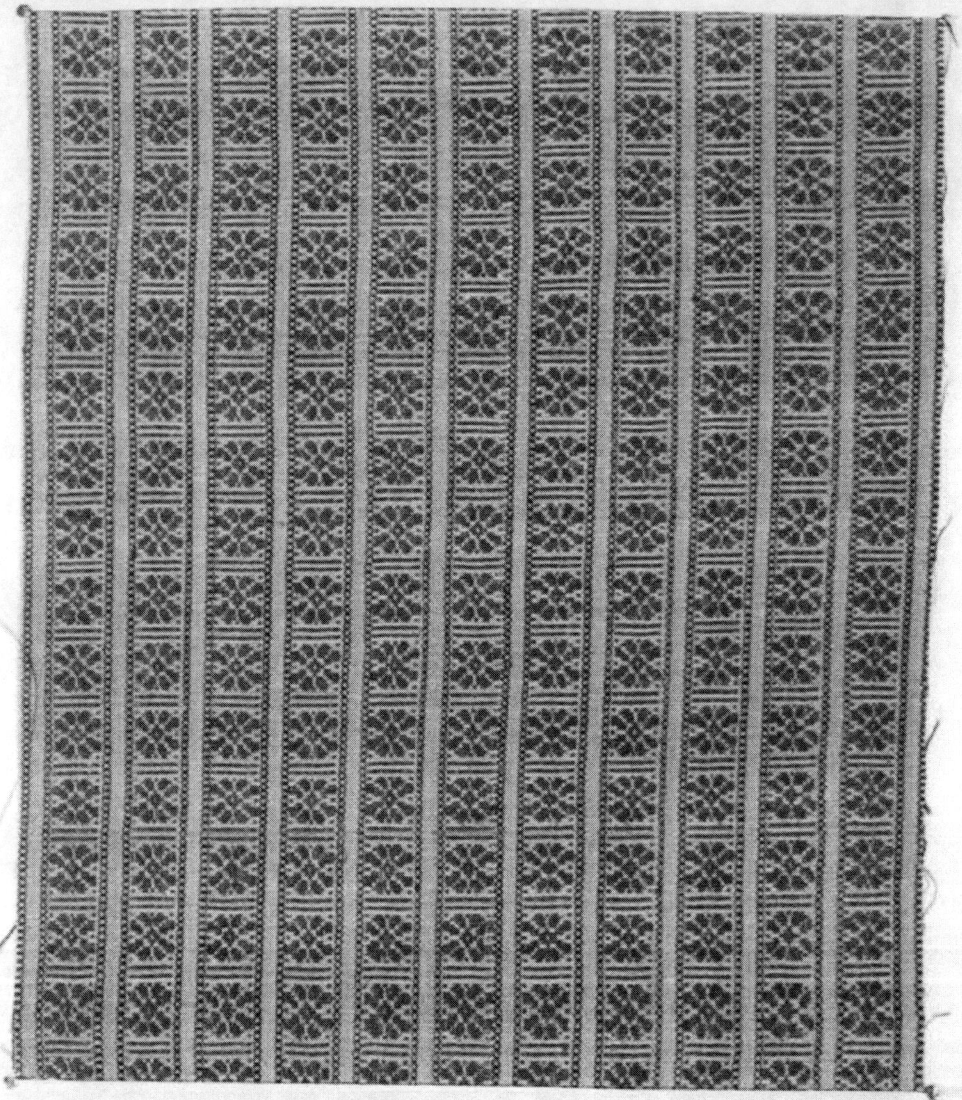

~~Prov. No. 337.~~ No. 535

INDIA FABRICS.

SILK PIECE GOODS.

Silk for dresses.

Length 15 yards; width 1 yard. Weight 1 lb. 10¼ oz.

From BHAGULPORE; BENGAL.

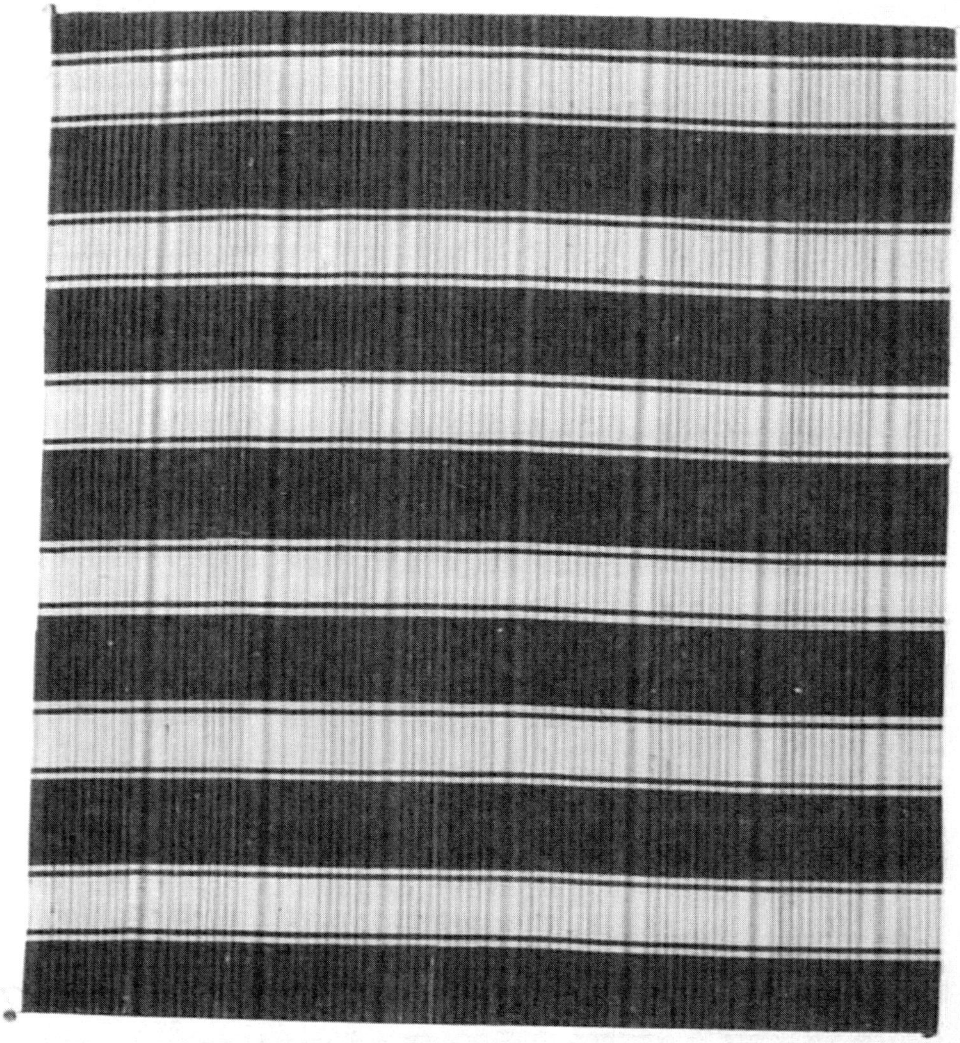

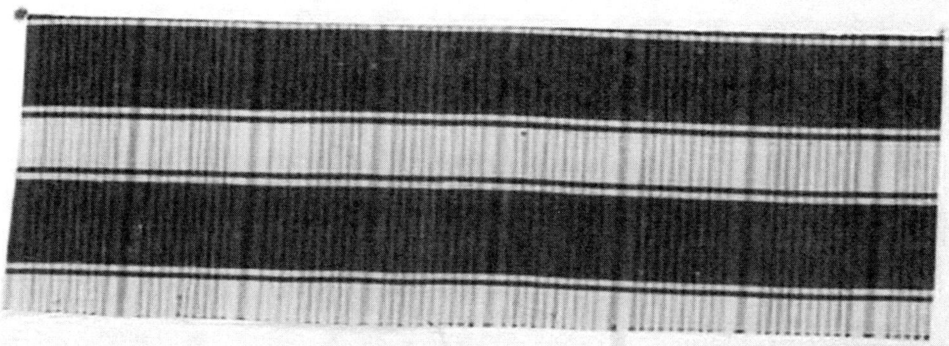

~~Prov. No. 549.~~ No. 536

INDIA FABRICS.

SILK PIECE GOODS.

Silk (check) for dresses. Good quality.

Length 15 yards; width 1 yard. Weight 1 lb. 10 oz.

From BERHAMPORE; BENGAL.

~~Prov. No. 555.~~ No. 537

INDIA FABRICS.

SILK PIECE GOODS.

Striped silk.

Length 5 yards 18 inches; width 31½ inches. Weight 11½ oz.

From BHAWULPORE: PUNJAB.

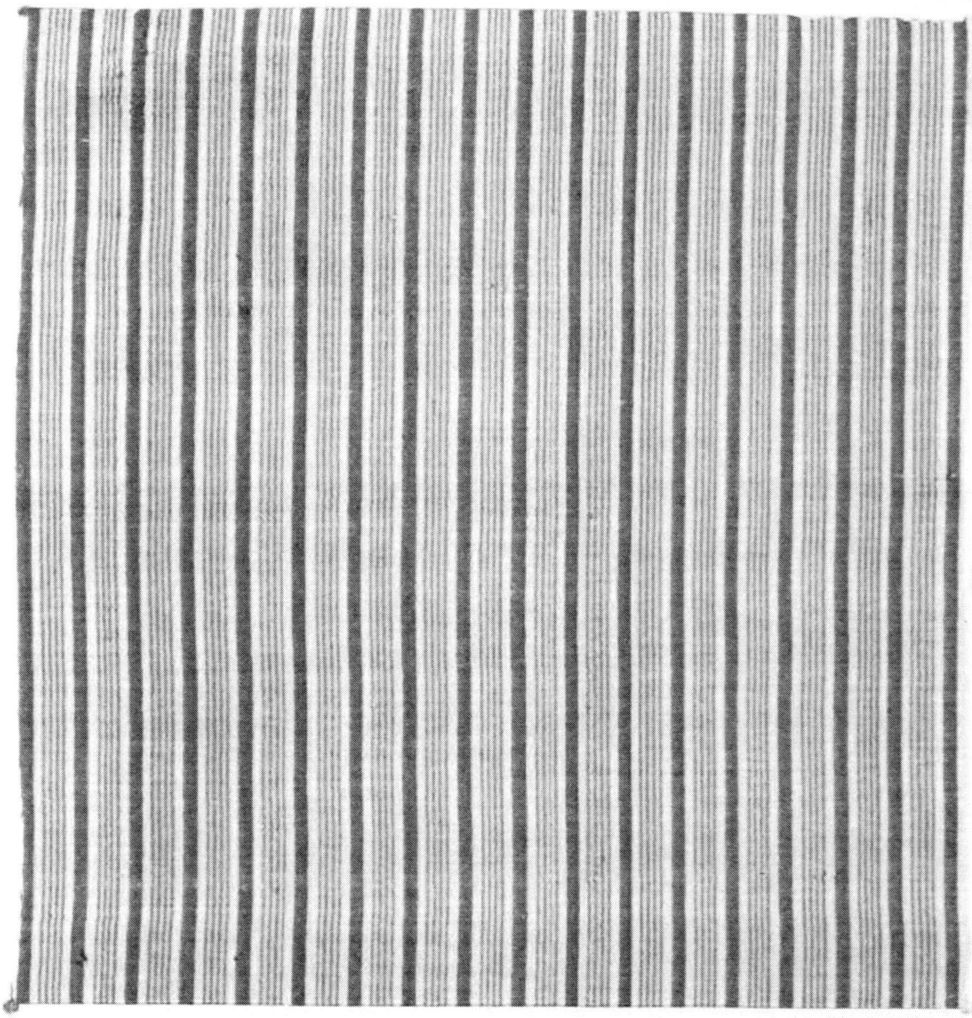

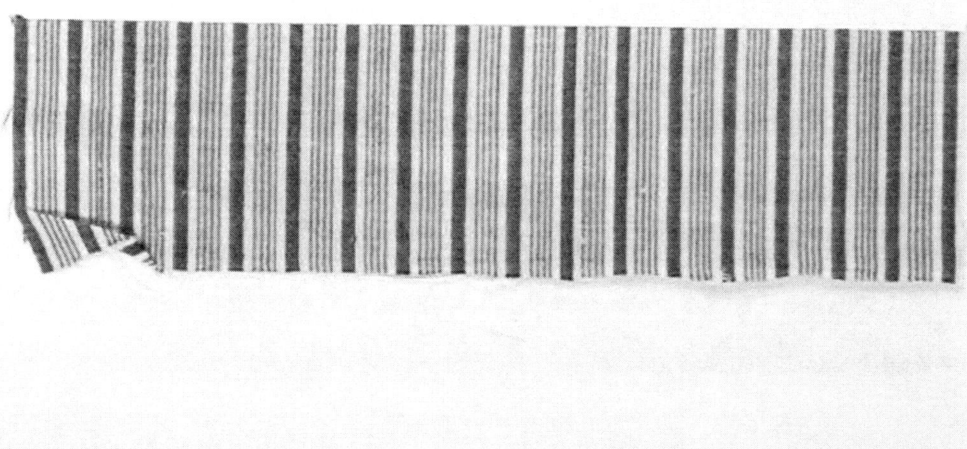

~~Prov. No. 666.~~ No. 538

INDIA FABRICS.

SILK PIECE GOODS.

Striped silk (Elaiche).

Length 19 yards 11 inches; width 19 inches. Weight 1 lb. 5 oz. Price 1*l.* 14*s.*

From AGRA; BENGAL.

~~Prov. No. 546.~~ No. 539

INDIA FABRICS.

SILK PIECE GOODS.

Silk (Durreeaee or striped) in colors.

Length 14 yards 14 inches ; width 11 inches. Weight 6¼ oz. Price 10s. 6d.

From AGRA ; BENGAL.

~~Prov. No. 534.~~ No. 540

INDIA FABRICS.

SILK PIECE GOODS.

Pink silk (Yeolah). Thin in texture and extra wide.

Length 11 yards; width 1 yard 5 inches. Weight 1 lb. 3 oz. Price 5l. 7s. 5d.

From AHMEDNUGGUR; BOMBAY.

~~Prov. No. 555.~~ No. 541

INDIA FABRICS.

SILK PIECE GOODS.

Yellow silk (Durreeaee). Very narrow.

Length 39 yards 18 inches; width 11½ inches. Weight 1 lb. ¾ oz. Price 1*l.* 9*s.* 8¼*d.*

From AGRA; BENGAL.

~~Prov. No. 547.~~ No. 542

INDIA FABRICS.

SILK PIECE GOODS.

Silk (and cotton). Small check.

Length 10 yards 18 inches; width 28 inches. Weight 1 lb. 6½ oz.

From AGRA; BENGAL.

No. 543

INDIA FABRICS.

SILK PIECE GOODS.

Silk for garments, used by men and women.

A peculiar fabric, woven with stripes at centre and ends; to be cut in two and sewn together at sides to form a garment.

Length 8 yards 28 inches; width $24\frac{1}{4}$ inches. Weight 1 lb. $1\frac{1}{2}$ oz. When cut for wear, 4 yards 14 inches long.

From PEGU; BURMAH.

~~Prov. No. 588.~~ No. 544

INDIA FABRICS.

SILK PIECE GOODS.

Used for garments by both men and women.

THE PIECE IS CUT IN TWO FOR WEAR, AND SEWN TOGETHER AT SIDES.

Full length 8 yards 28 inches; width 25½ inches. Weight 1 lb. 2¼ oz.

From PEGU; BURMAH.

~~Prov. No. 542.~~ No. 545

INDIA FABRICS.

SILK PIECE GOODS.

Used for garments by both men and women.

THE LENGTH IS CUT IN TWO, AND FOR WEAR SEWN TOGETHER AT SIDES.

Full length 8 yards 30 inches; width 25 inches. Weight 1 lb. 4 oz.

From PEGU; BURMAH.

~~Prev. No. 542.~~ No. 546

INDIA FABRICS.

SILK PIECE GOODS.

Silk for garments, with colored stripes.

This piece is 8 yards 26 inches long by 27½ inches wide. Weight 1 lb. 1½ oz.

From PEGU; BURMAH.

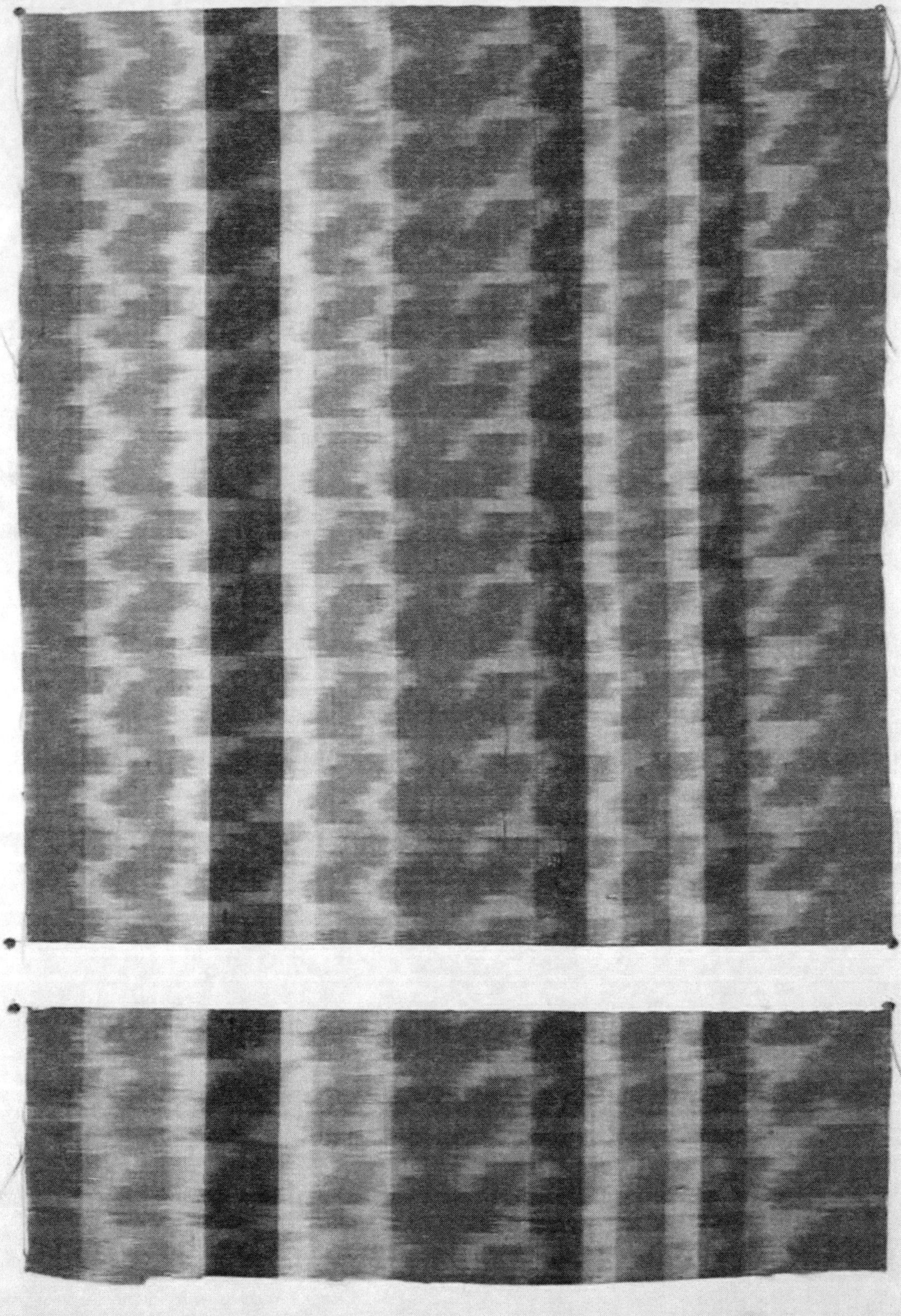

~~Prev. No. 546.~~ No. 541

INDIA FABRICS.

SILK PIECE GOODS.

Silk piece for garments.

This piece is 9 yards long by 24 inches wide. Weight 1 lb. 13¼ oz.

From PEGU; BURMAH.

~~Prov. No. 588.~~ No. 548

INDIA FABRICS.

HANDKERCHIEFS.

Silk kerchiefs ("Lahe Meenia.")

PATTERN USED BY PARSEES.

Length 1 yard 11 inches; width 1 yard 21 inches. Weight $5\frac{1}{2}$ oz. Price 6s.

From SURAT; BOMBAY.

~~Piece No. 550.~~

No. 549

INDIA FABRICS.

HANDKERCHIEFS.

Silk kerchiefs (black "Lahe"), used by Parsees.

Length 1 yard 10 inches; width 29 inches. Weight 1½ oz. Price 6s.

From SURAT; BOMBAY.

~~Prov. No 661.~~ No. 550

INDIA FABRICS.

HANDKERCHIEFS.

Silk handkerchief in colors.

PATTERN USED BY PARSEES.

31½ inches by 30 inches. Weight 2 oz. Price 3s.

From SURAT; BOMBAY.

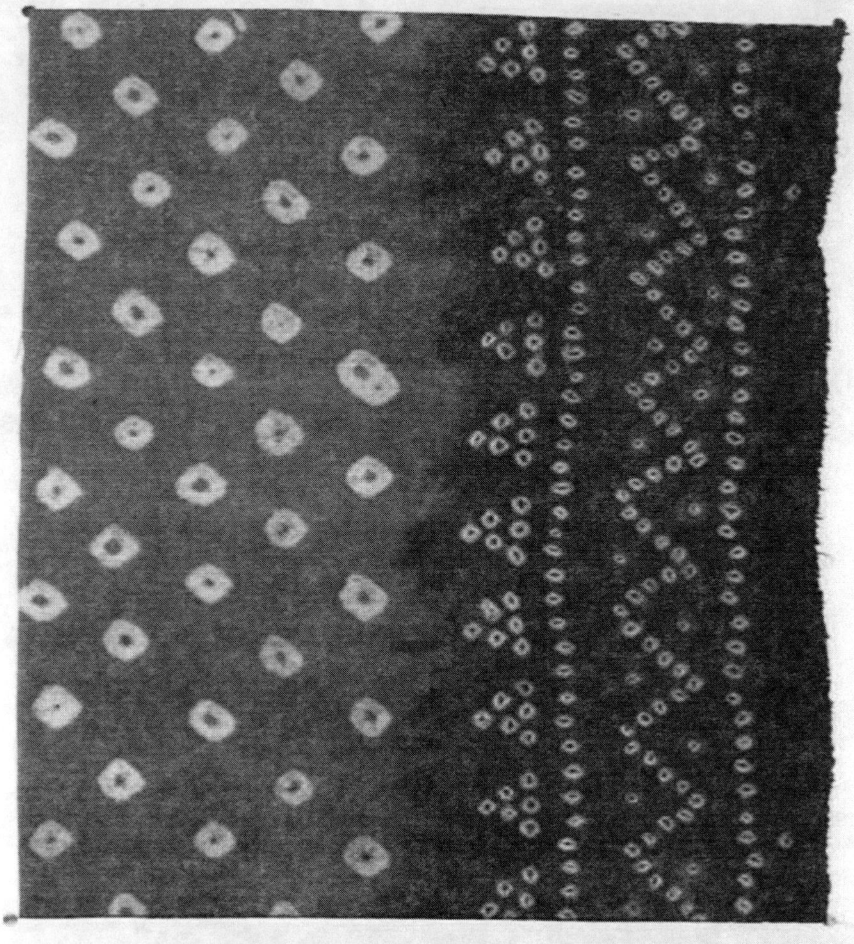

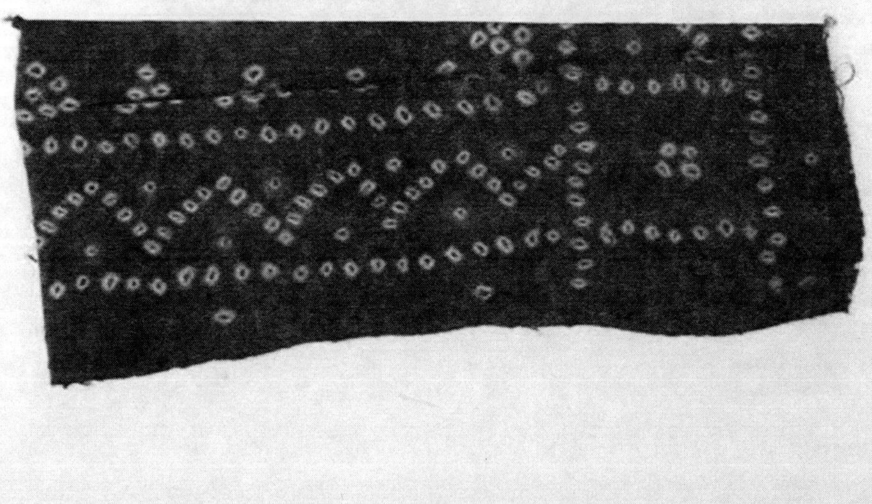

~~Prov. No. 660.~~ No. 551

INDIA FABRICS.

HANDKERCHIEFS.

Silk handkerchief, called "printed Lahe."

32 inches in length ; 31 inches in width. Weight 2 oz. Price 5s. 3d.

From SURAT ; BOMBAY.

~~Prov. No. 568.~~ No. 552

INDIA FABRICS.

SILK GAUZE.

Silk gauze with gold flowers.

Length 8 yards; width 1 yard. Weight 6½ oz. Price 19s.

From TRICHINOPOLY; MADRAS.

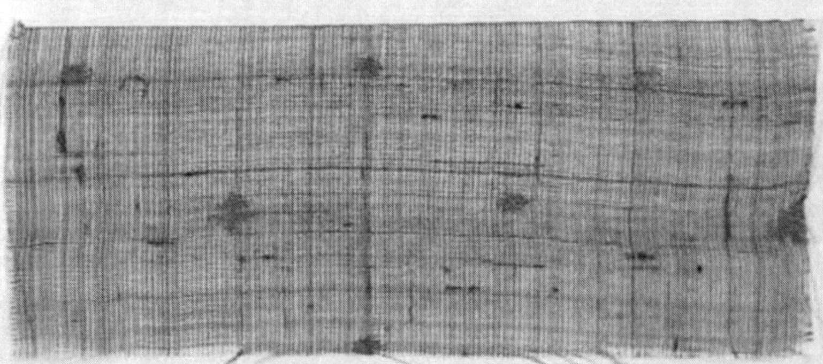

~~Prov. No. 666.~~ No. 553

INDIA FABRICS.

SILK GAUZE.

Silk gauze with gold flowers.

Length 8 yards; width 34 inches. Weight 6¾ oz. Price 19s.

From TRICHINOPOLY; MADRAS.

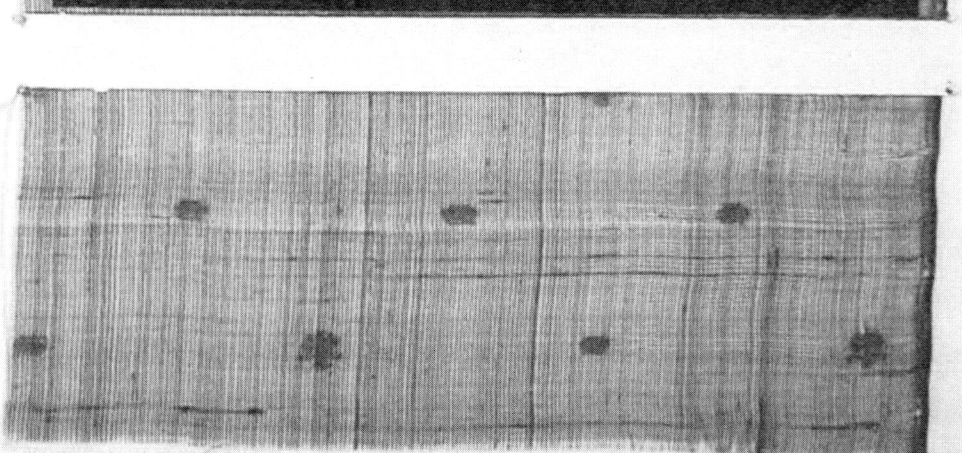

~~Prov. No. 564.~~ No. 554

INDIA FABRICS.

SILK GAUZE.

Silk gauze with gold flowers.

Length 8 yards; width 1 yard. Weight 5¾ oz. Price 19s.

From TRICHINOPOLY; MADRAS.

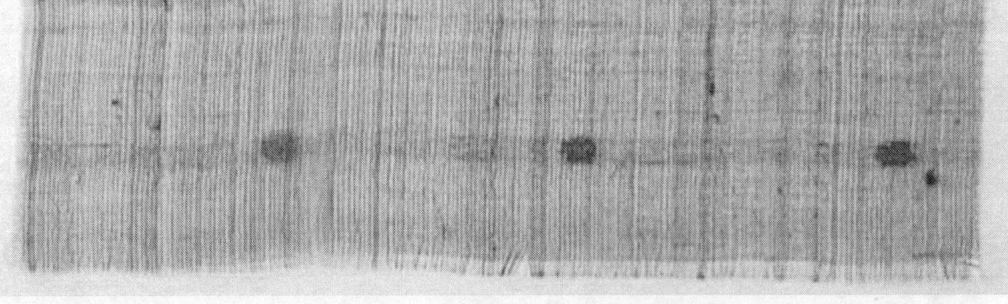

~~Prov. No. 662.~~ No. 555

INDIA FABRICS.

SILK GAUZE.

Silk gauze used for musquito curtains.

Length 11 yards; width 31 inches. Weight $5\frac{3}{4}$ oz. Price 1*l.* 12*s.*

From BHAGULPORE: BENGAL.

~~Prov. No. 368.~~ No. 556

INDIA FABRICS.

TUSSUR SILK.

Tussur silk. Plain.

Length 10 yards 18 inches; width 1 yard 1 inch. Weight 1 lb. 15½ oz. Price 15s. 10½d.

From WARUNGUL, HYDERABAD; DECCAN.

~~Prov. No. [illegible]~~

No. 557

INDIA FABRICS.

TUSSUR SILK.

Tussur silk (twilled). Dyed.

Length 11 yards ; width 26 inches. Weight 1 lb. 7½ oz. Price 13s.

From BHAGULPORE ; BENGAL.

~~Prov. No. 546.~~ No. 558

INDIA FABRICS.

TUSSUR SILK.

Tussur silk, large check. Dyed.

Length 9 yards 18 inches; width 25¼ inches. Weight 1 lb. 4 oz. Price 13s.

From BHAGULPORE; BENGAL.

~~Prov. No. 669.~~

No. 559

INDIA FABRICS.

ERIA SILK.

Eria silk piece, named "Dooklee": coarse.

Length 4 yards; width 34 inches. Weight 1 lb. 6 oz. Price 4s.

From CACHAR; BENGAL.

~~Prov. No. 567.~~ No. 560

INDIA FABRICS.

ERIA SILK.

Eria (wild) silk. Piece named "Endi," cloth.

USED FOR GARMENTS BY MEN AND WOMEN.

Length 3 yards 2 inches ; width 1 yard 4 inches. Weight 1 lb. 4 oz.

From DARJEELING.

THE TEXTILE MANUFACTURERS OF INDIA

JOHN FORBES WATSON

VOLUME:-15

1866

~~Prov. Nos. 630 and 636 A.~~ No. 561 / 562

ASIATIC FABRICS.

SILK AND COTTON.

No. 1. Mixed material, called "Uddrussa," (full pattern shown in this sample.)

Length 7 yards; width 11½ inches. Price 9s.

No. 2. Bordered fabric; yellow borders and ends.

Width of piece with single border 25 inches.

Manufactured in BOKHARA.

561 562

~~Prov. No. 637.~~ No. 563

ASIATIC FABRICS.

COTTON AND SILK.

Cotton and Silk material, called "Uddrussa" in Bokhara and "Elacha" in Sind.

USED FOR LININGS OF COATS. FULL PATTERN SHOWN IN HALF PIECE.

Length 7 yards 9 inches; width 12 inches. Price 11s.

Manufactured in BOKHARA.

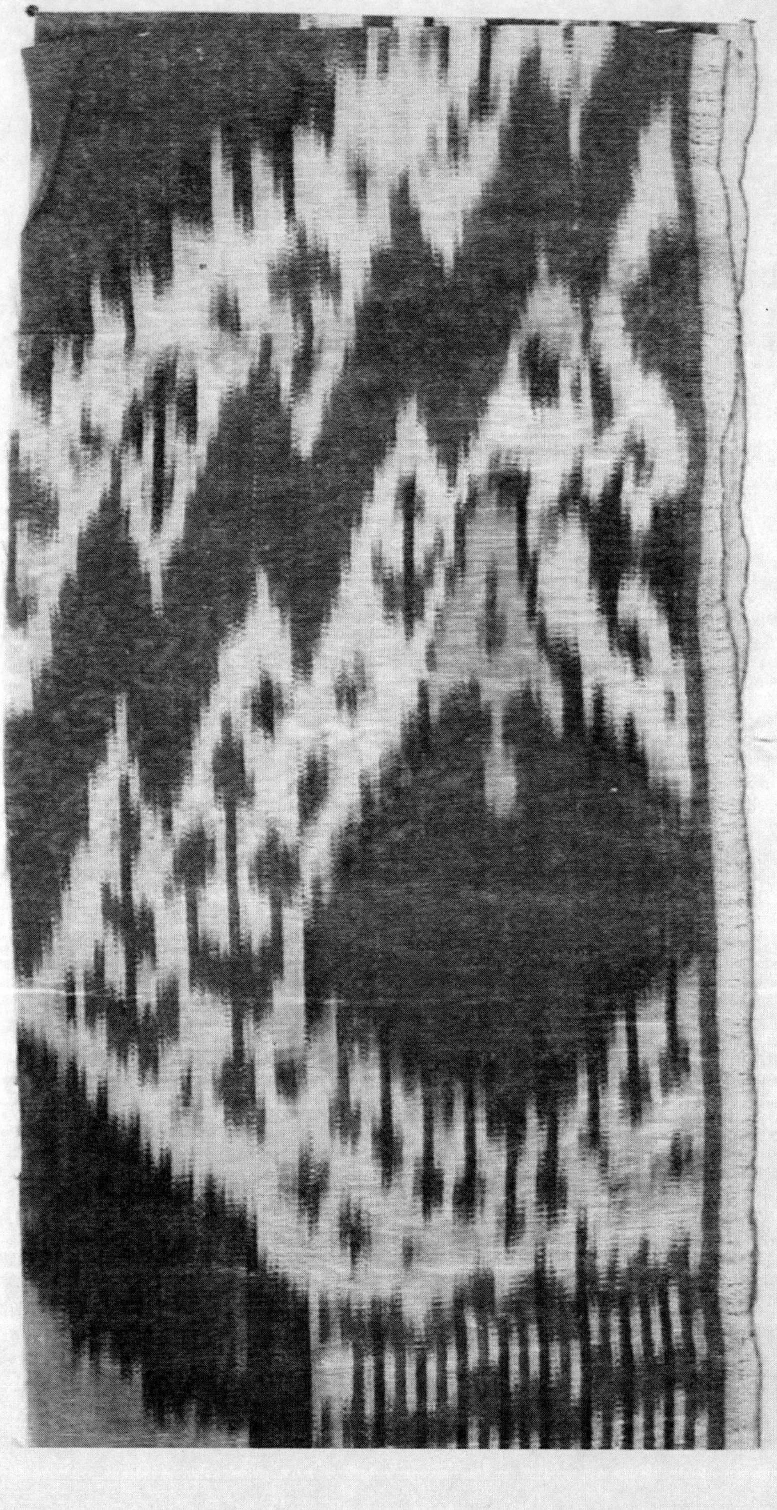

Prov. No. 640. No. 564

ASIATIC FABRICS.

SILK AND COTTON.

Mixed material, called " Uddrussa " in Bokhara and " Elacha " in Scind.

CUT CROSSWAYS TO SHOW FULL PATTERN. MUCH PRIZED AND SOUGHT AFTER.

Length 3 yards 16 inches; width 19½ inches. Price 13s.

Manufactured in BOKHARA.

Prov. No. 641. No. 565

ASIATIC FABRICS.

SILK AND COTTON.

Mixed material called "Ulukh."

SAMPLE (ONLY ONE THIRD THE PROPER WIDTH) SHOWS FULL PATTERN.

Length 3 yards 6 inches; width 20½ inches. Price 10s.

Manufactured in BOKHARA.

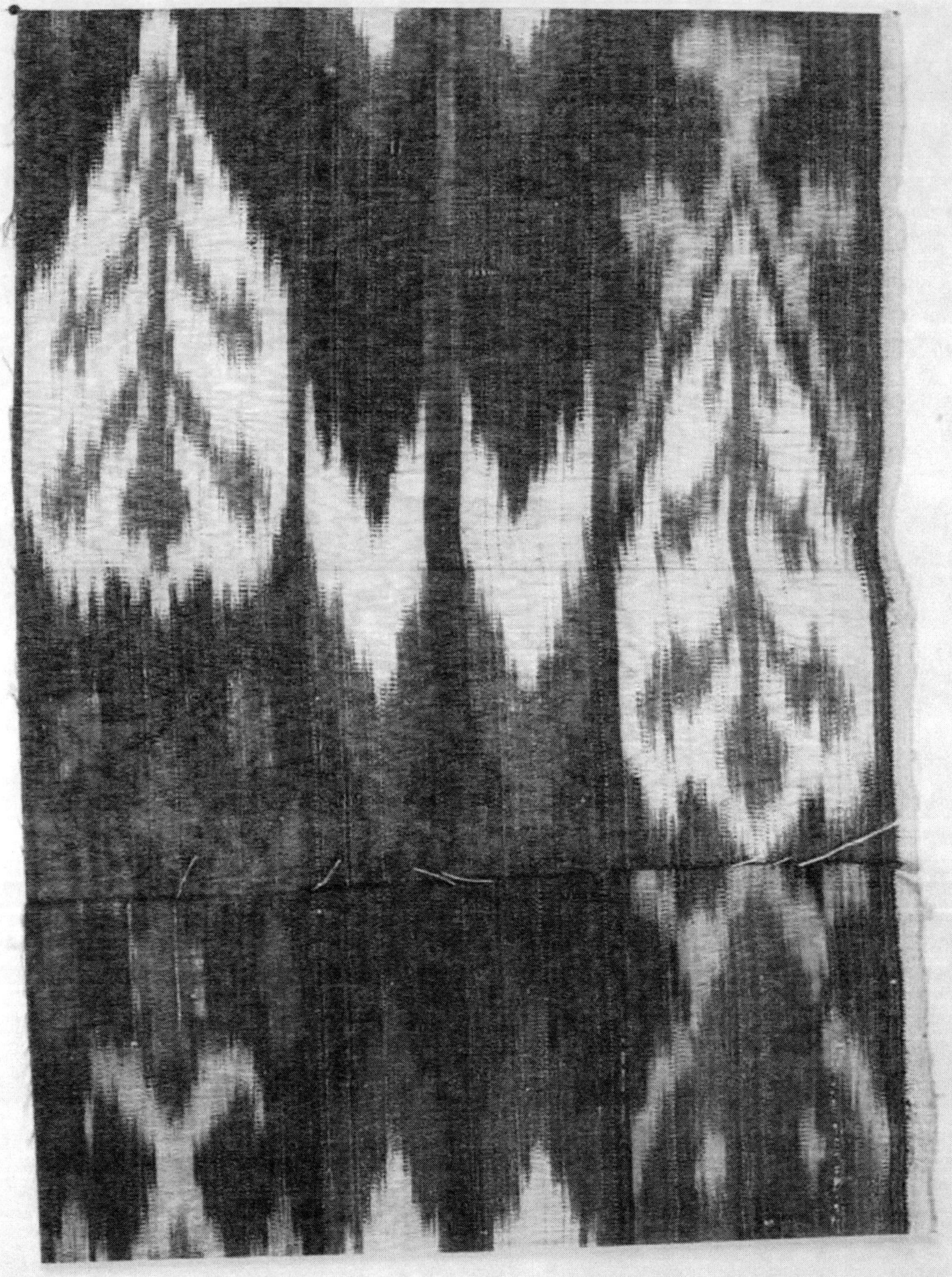

Prov. Nos. 669 and 635.

No. {566, 567}

ASIATIC FABRICS.

SILK.

No. 1. Striped silk piece, called "Goolbuddan."

Length 32 inches; width 29 inches. Price about 2s. 10d.

No. 2. Siik bordered piece for a garment.

Width of piece, with border on one side only, 26 inches.

Manufactured in BOKHARA.

566

567

Prov. No. 638. No. 568

ASIATIC FABRICS.

SILK AND COTTON.

Mixed material, called "Bakisum" and "Elacha."

Full pattern in sample. To be obtained in Cashmere down to Kurrachee.

Length about 5 yards; width 12½ inches. Price about 12s.

Manufactured in BOKHARA.

~~Prov. Nos. 642 and 643.~~ No. {569 570}

ASIATIC FABRICS.

CHINTZES.

No. 1. Glazed cotton chintz called "Kootnee."

IN PRETTY GENERAL USE. FULL PATTERN IN SAMPLE.

Length 3 yards 18 inches; width 21½ inches. Price 8s.

No. 2. Glazed cotton piece, cut crossways.

Width 11 inches.

Manufactured in BOKHARA?

569

570

~~Prov. No. 644.~~ No. 571 A B

ASIATIC FABRICS.

SILKS.

Silk material, called "Khoodbauf." Of two colors.

USED BY NATIVES OF THE UPPER CLASSES.

Length 1 yard; width 29 inches. Price 4s. 6d.

Manufactured at BOKHARA; *obtained in* SCIND.

571 A 571 B

~~Prov. Nos. 645 and 668.~~ No. 572 A B / 573

ASIATIC FABRICS.

COTTON MATERIAL.

No. 1. Glazed cotton or chintz; two samples; striped.

Width of each piece 20 inches.

No. 2. Green cotton piece; plain. Called "Nauker."

Width 14 inches.

Manufactured in BOKHARA.

~~Prov. No. 636.~~ No. 574

ASIATIC FABRICS.

SILKS.

Striped silk, bordered, called "Goolbuddan."

CUT CROSSWAYS OF THE PIECE TO GIVE FULL PATTERN.

Length 32 inches; width 25 inches. Price of piece 3s. 11d.

Manufactured in BOKHARA.

~~Prov. No. 670.~~

No. { 575
576

ASIATIC FABRICS.

SILKS.

Plain silks of two colors, called "Kunawey."

Length of each piece 30 inches; width 27½ inches. Price 2s. 7½d.

Manufactured in BOKHARA.

575 576

~~Prov. No. 671.~~ No. 577 / 578

ASIATIC FABRICS.

SILKS.

Plain silk pieces of two colors, called "Kunawey."

Length of each piece 30 inches; width 27½ inches. Price 2s. 7½d.

Manufactured in BOKHARA.

577 578

~~Prov. No. 672.~~

No. 579, 580

ASIATIC FABRICS.

SILKS.

Plain silk pieces of two colors, called "Kunawey."

Length of each piece 30 inches; width 27½ inches. Price 2s. 7½d.

Manufactured in BOKHARA.

579

580

Prov. No. 673. No. 581 / 582

ASIATIC FABRICS.

SILKS.

Plain silk pieces of two colors, called "Kunawey."

Length of each piece 30 inches; width $27\frac{1}{2}$ inches. Price 2s. $7\frac{1}{2}$d.

Manufactured in BOKHARA.

581 582

Prov. No. 660. No. { 583 / 584

ASIATIC FABRICS.

SILKS.

Figured silk gauze of two colors, called " Boolbool Chrshum."

Width of yellow 28 inches ; width of white 21 inches.

Manufactured at MESHED.

583 584

~~Prov. No. 661.~~ No. {585 / 586}

ASIATIC FABRICS.

SILKS.

Figured silk of two colors, called "Boolbool Chrshum."

Width of green (shot) 15 inches; of pink 24 inches. Price per yard about 3s. 6d.

Manufactured at MESHED.

585

586

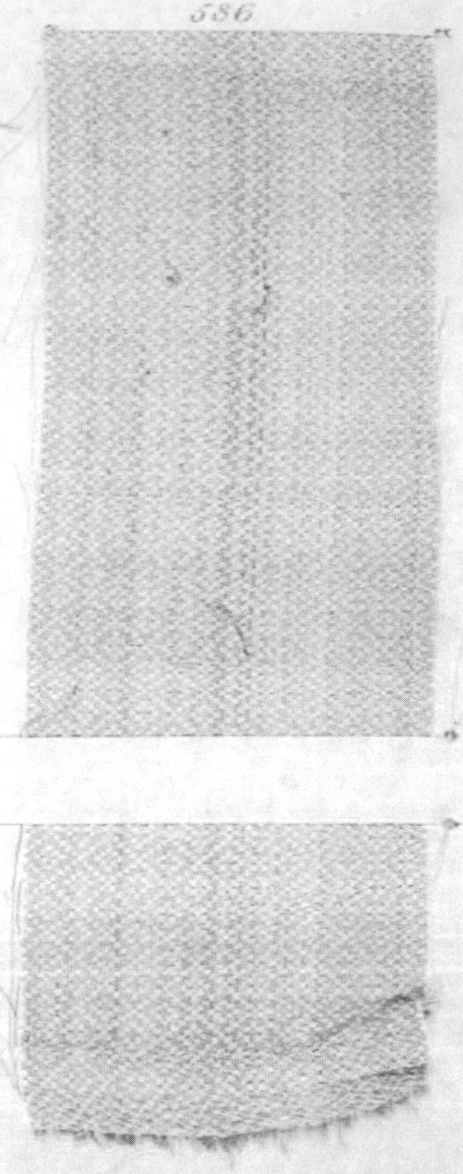

~~Prov. No. 662.~~ No. 587

ASIATIC FABRICS.

SILKS.

Blue and crimson figured silk.

Width 16 inches. No price affixed.

Manufactured in MESHED.

~~Prov. No. 668.~~ No. { 588 / 589

ASIATIC FABRICS.

SILKS.

Colored striped silk piece.

Width 20 inches.

Yellow and crimson figured silk piece.

Width 18 inches.

Manufactured in MESHED.

~~Prov. No. 664.~~ No. { 590 / 591 }

ASIATIC FABRICS.

SILKS.

Figured silk pieces of two colors, called "Musjoor."

Width of each 18 inches. No price received.

Manufactured at MESHED.

590 591

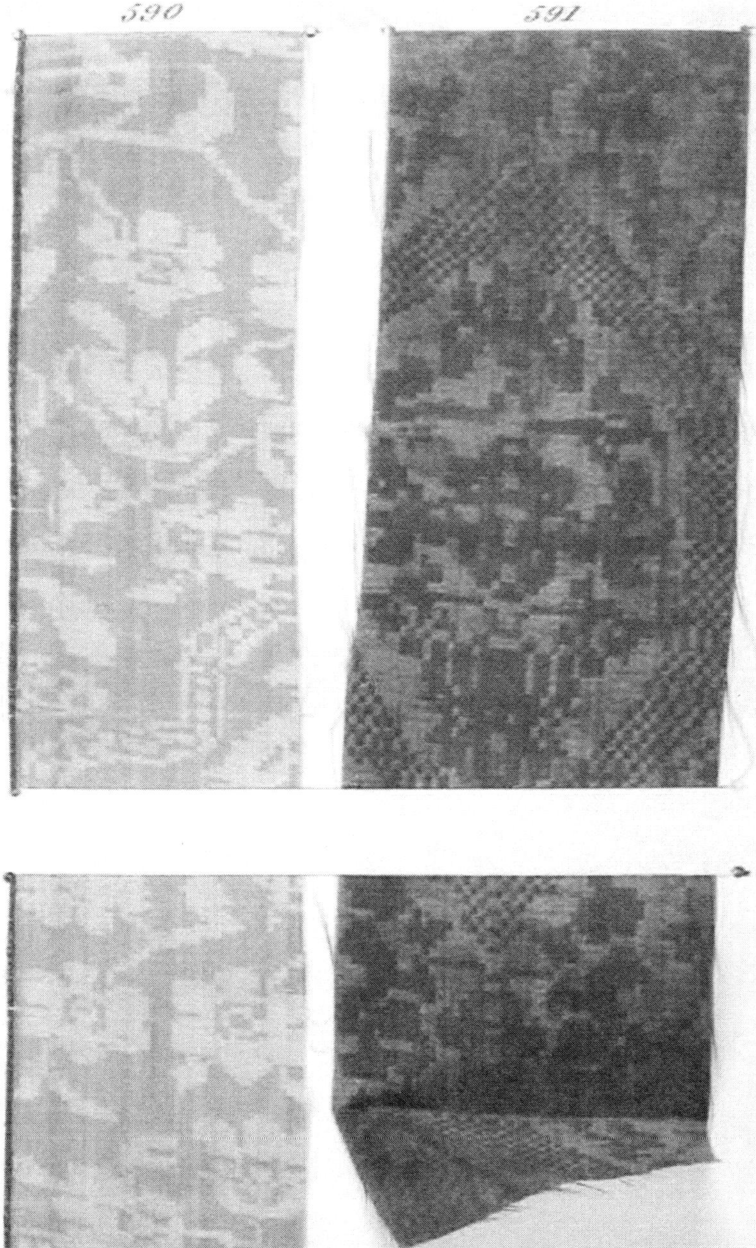

~~Prov. No. 665.~~ No. { 592 / 593

ASIATIC FABRICS.

SILKS.

Silk gauze stripes and flowers of two colors.

Width of each piece 24 inches.

Manufactured in MESHED.

592

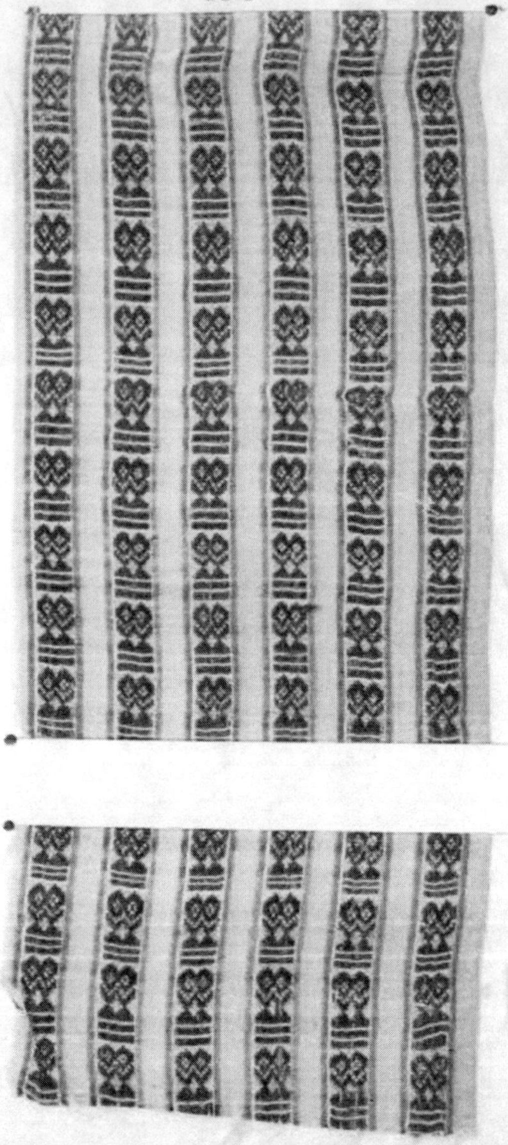

593

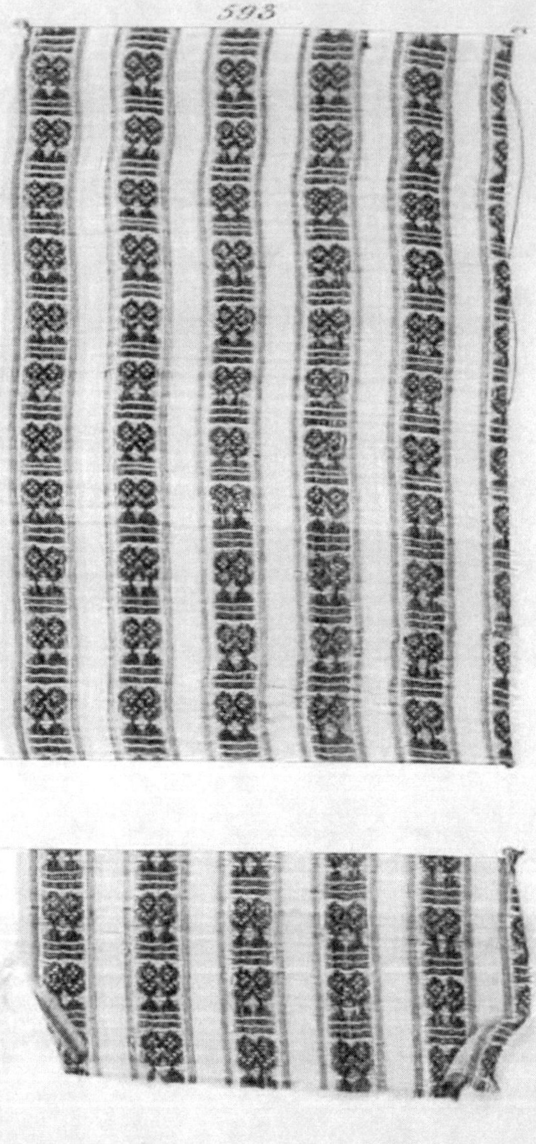

~~Prov. No. 647.~~ No. 594

ASIATIC FABRICS.

SHAWL PATTERNS.

Figured silk cloth called " Ubra " or " Shalwal."

USED FOR CHOGAS AND OTHER GARMENTS.

Width 25½ inches. Price 10s. per yard.

Manufactured in HERAT.

~~Prov. No. 648.~~ No. 595

ASIATIC FABRICS.

SHAWL PATTERN.

Figured silk cloth called "Ubra" or "Shalwal."

USED FOR CHOGAS AND OTHER GARMENTS.

Width 25½ inches. Price 10s. per yard.

Manufactured in HERAT.

~~Prov. No. 649.~~ No. 596

ASIATIC FABRICS.

SHAWL PATTERNS.

Figured silk cloth, called "Ubra" or "Shalwal?"

USED FOR CHOGAS AND OTHER GARMENTS.

Width 25½ inches. Price 10s. per yard.

Manufactured in HERAT.

Prov. No. 650. No. 597

ASIATIC FABRICS.

SHAWL PATTERN.

Figured silk cloth, called "Ubra" or "Shalwal."

USED FOR CHOGAS AND GARMENTS OF VARIOUS KINDS.

Width 25½ inches. Price 10s. per yard.

Manufactured in HERAT.

~~Prov. No. 651.~~ No. 598

ASIATIC FABRICS.

SHAWL PATTERNS.

Figured silk cloth, called " Ubra " or " Shalwal?"

USED FOR CHOGAS AND GARMENTS OF VARIOUS KINDS.

Width 25¼ inches. Price 10s. per yard.

Manufactured in HERAT.

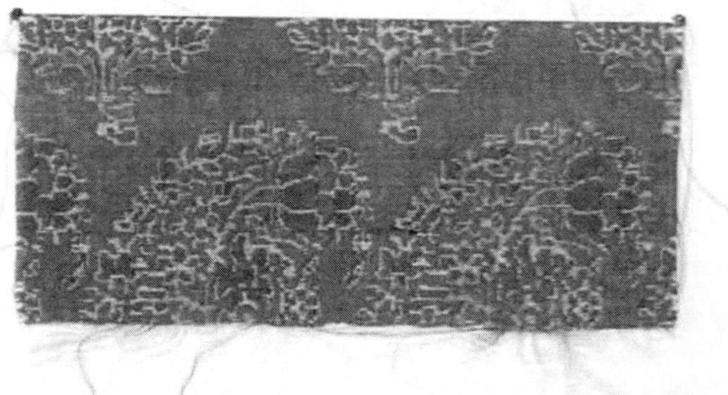

~~Prov. No. 652.~~

No. 599, 600

ASIATIC FABRICS.

COTTON AND SILK.

Satin, called "Atlas," of two colors.

Width of red 29 inches; width of black 17½ inches.

Manufactured in HERAT.

599 600

~~Prov. No. 650.~~

No. { 601 / 602

ASIATIC FABRICS.

No. 1. Brown cotton cloth, called " Naukrr."

Width 17 inches.

No. 2. Yellow satin, called " Atlas." Cotton back.

Width 28 inches.

Manufactured in HERAT.

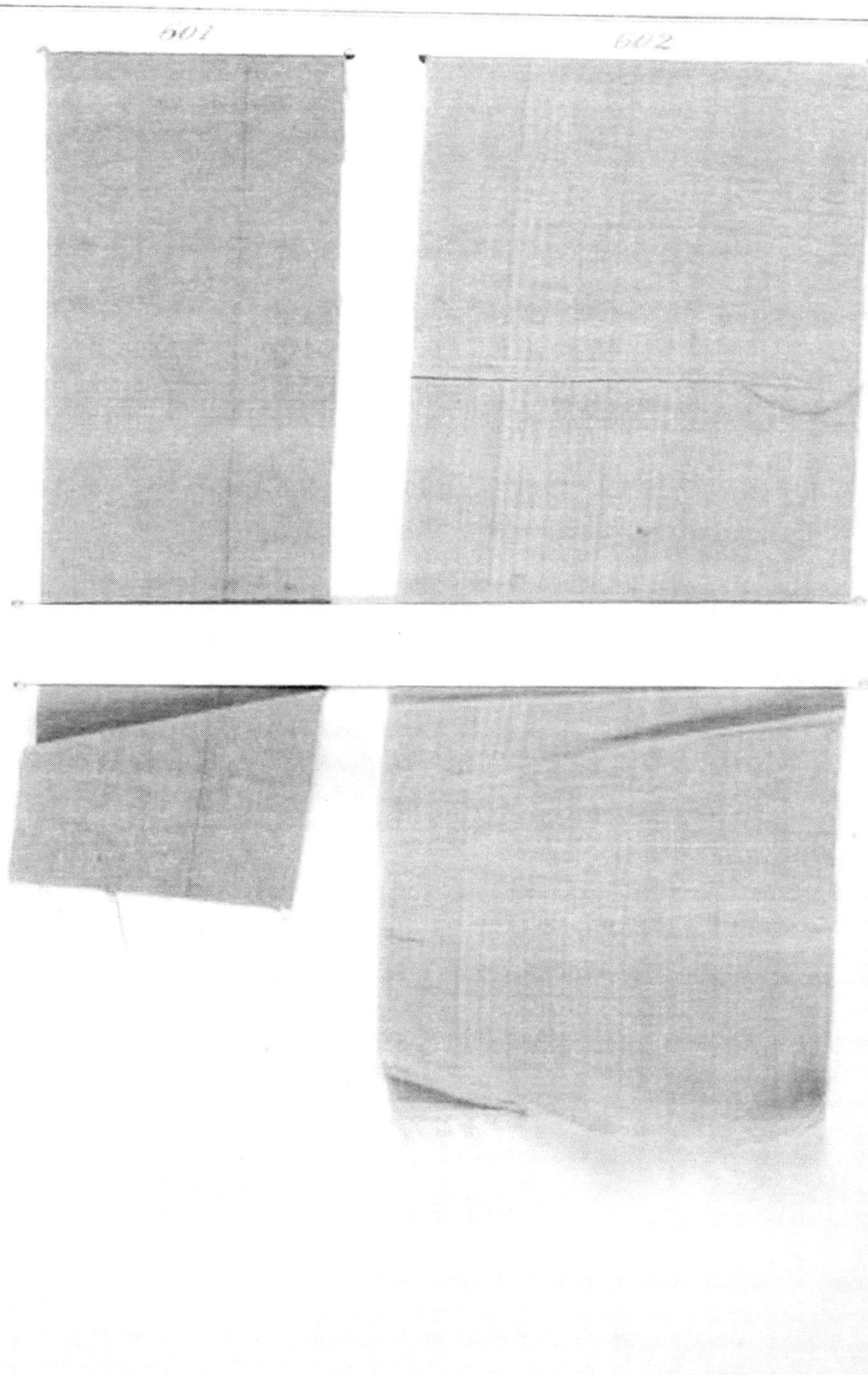

~~Prov. No. 646.~~ No. 603

ASIATIC FABRICS.

SILKS.

Silk piece, called "Goolbuddun."

Width 18 inches.

Manufacture of YEZD.

~~Prov. No. 684.~~ No. *604*

ASIATIC FABRICS.

SILK.

Silk brocade.

Width 29 inches. Price about 4s. per yard.

Manufactured in BALK.

~~Prov. No. 656.~~ No. 605

ASIATIC FABRICS.

SILKS.

Silk brocade.

Width 29½ inches. Price about 4s. per yard.

Manufactured in BALK.

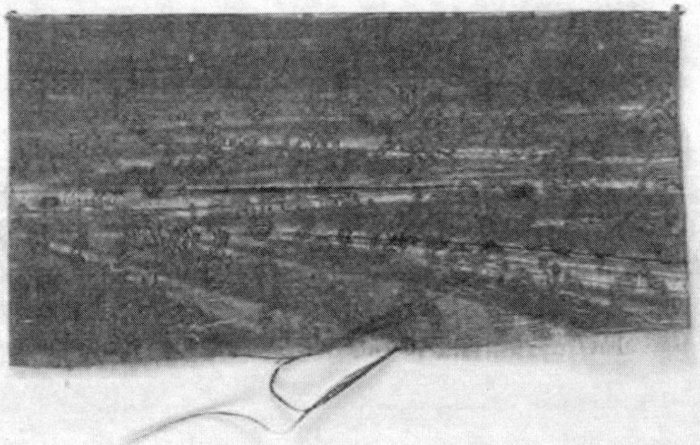

~~Prov. Nos. 656.~~ No. { 606 607

ASIATIC FABRICS.

SILKS.

Figured silk, two samples, called " Boodul."

MUCH USED IN LADAK.

Width of each piece varying from 9 to 17 inches. Price about 2s. per yard.

Manufactured in BALK.

606 607

~~Prov. Nos. 658 and 657.~~ No. { 608 / 609

ASIATIC FABRICS.

SILKS.

No. 1. Figured silk piece, flimsy material, called "Boodul."

Width 17 inches. Price about 2s. per yard.

No. 2. Figured silk, harsh on surface.

Width 19 inches.

Manufactured in BALK.

608

609

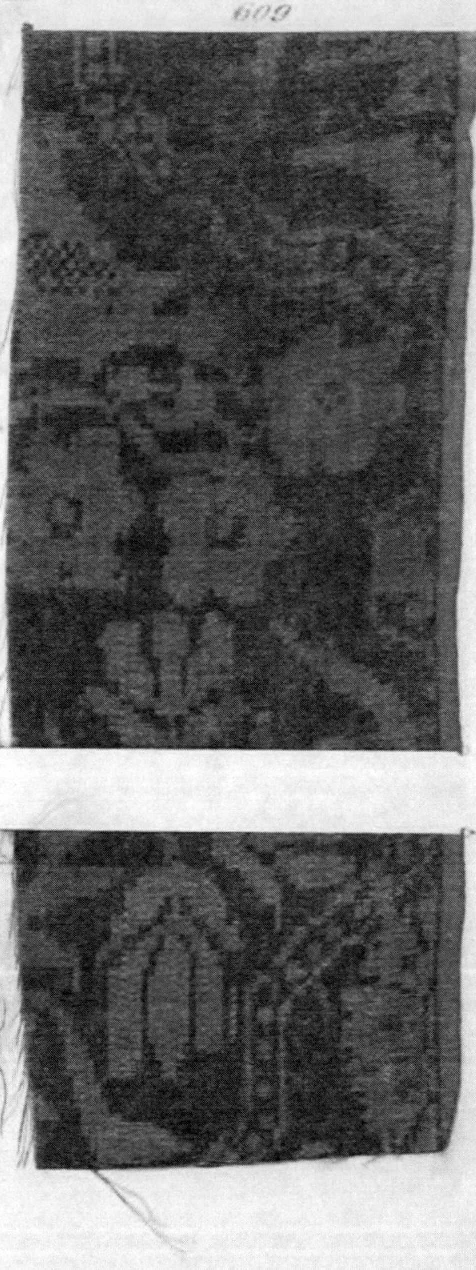

~~Prov. No. 659.~~ No. *610*

ASIATIC FABRICS.

SILKS.

Figured silk of peculiar design; pattern complete in sample.

Length 6 yards; width 25 inches. Price 13s.

Manufactured in BALK.

~~Prov. No. 667.~~ No. 611 / 612

ASIATIC FABRICS.

SILK.

No. 1. Silk gauze, with a little cotton.

No. 2. Gauze, silk only.

Width 28 inches.

Manufactured in KOKAN.

611 612

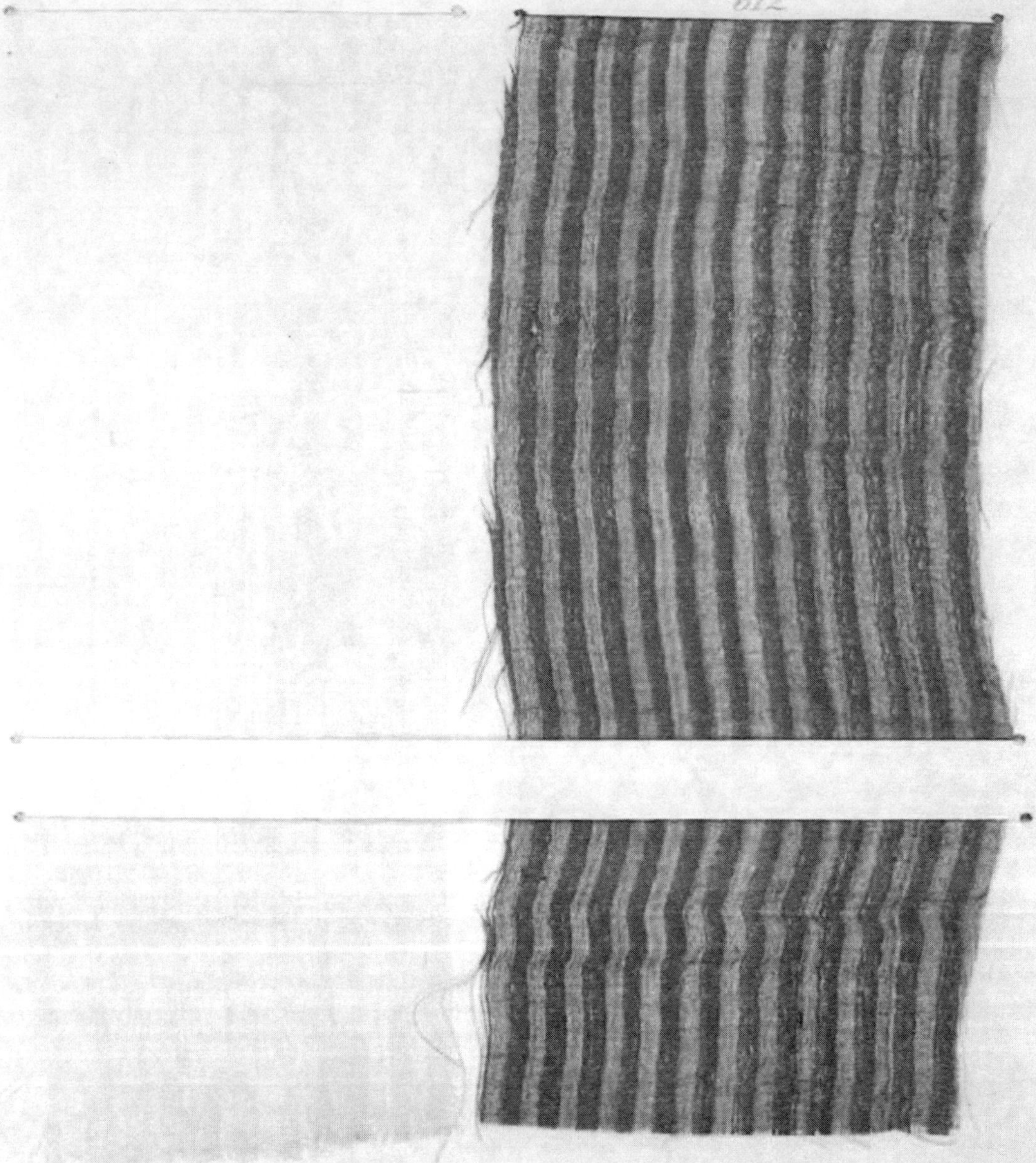

~~Prov. No. 666.~~ No. { 613 / 614

ASIATIC FABRICS.

SILK.

Striped silk gauze material, called "Dasija."

Length of each sample 30 inches; width 26 inches. Price 1s. 1½d. the piece.

Manufactured in KOKUR.

613

614

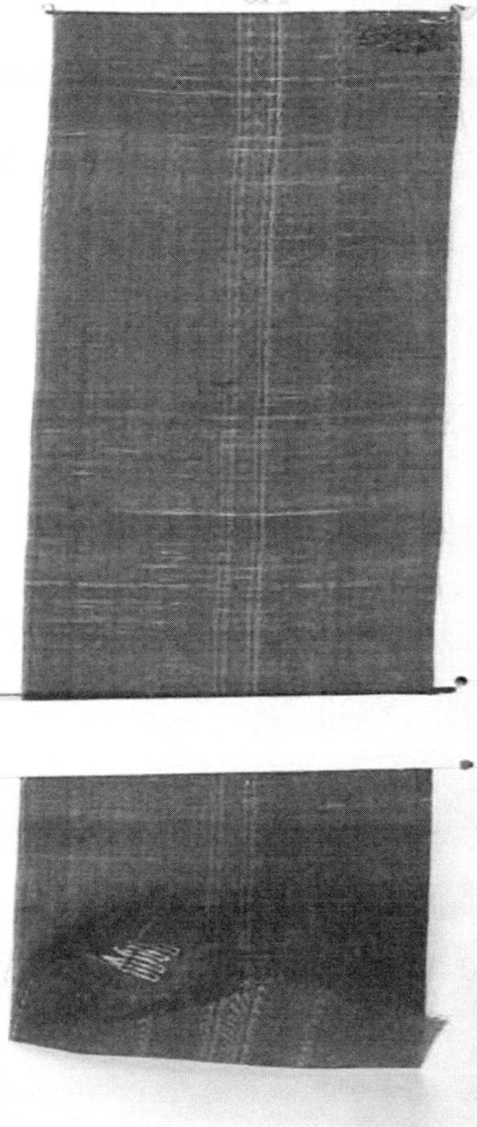

~~Prov. Nos. 674 and 675.~~ No. 615 / 616

ASIATIC FABRICS.

FIGURED SILKS.

No. 1. Blue figured silk, called "Saujoo Gool Goshen."

Width 30 inches.

Obtained in BOKHARA.

No. 2. Colored figured satin.

Length 31 inches; width 20 inches. Price 7s.

Obtained in BOKHARA; *manufactured in* RUSSIA.

615

616

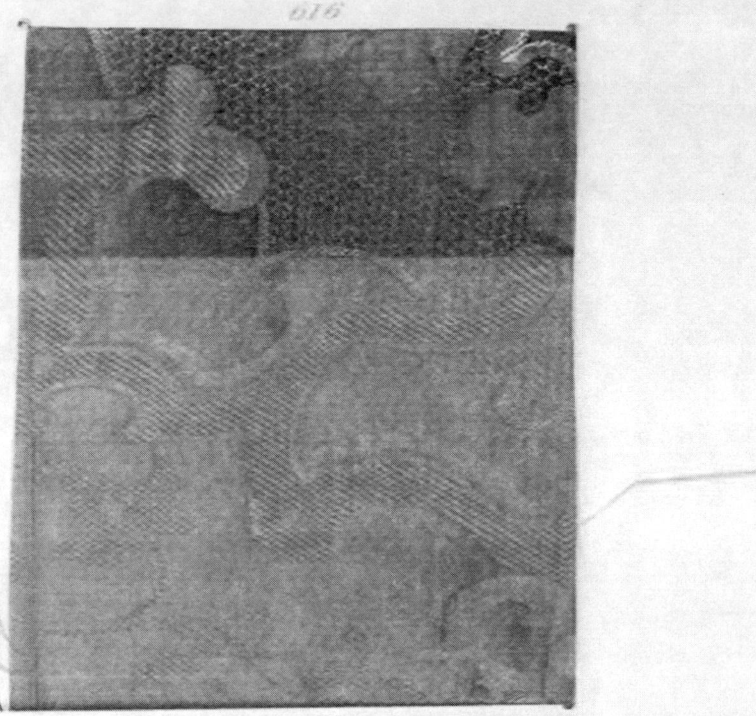

~~Prov. No. 676.~~ No. *617*

ASIATIC FABRICS.

SILK.

Figured satin; full pattern in sample.

Length 31 inches; width 29 inches. Price 7s.

Obtained in BOKHARA; *manufactured in* RUSSIA.

~~Prov. No. 677.~~

No. 618, 619

ASIATIC FABRICS.

FIGURED SILKS.

Figured satin; two samples.

CUT CROSSWAYS TO SECURE FULL PATTERN.

Length 31 inches; width 20 inches. Price 7s.

Obtained in BOKHARA; *manufactured in* RUSSIA.

618

619

~~Prov. No. 678.~~

No. 620, 621

ASIATIC FABRICS.

FIGURED SILK.

Satins; two samples.

CUT CROSSWAYS. FULL PATTERN GIVEN.

Length 31 inches; width 20 inches. Price 7s.

Obtained in BOKHARA; *manufactured in* RUSSIA.

620 621

~~Prov. No. 679.~~ No. { 622 / 623

ASIATIC FABRICS.

Woollen fabric of bright colors.

Width 33 inches.

Striped calico called "Naukrr."

Width 13 inches.

Obtained in BOKHARA ; *manufactured at* OOROOS *in* RUSSIA.

622

623

THE TEXTILE MANUFACTURERS OF INDIA

JOHN FORBES WATSON

VOLUME:- 16

1866

~~Prov. No. 691.~~

No. 624

INDIA FABRICS.

WOOLLENS.

" Kooroon " or " Sulung " cloth. Fine quality.

PRICE IN CASHMERE ABOUT 2*s.* 3*d.* PER YARD.

Length of piece 20 yards ; width 16½ inches. Weight 3 lbs. 2 oz.

Made in SULUNG, *between* LASSA *and* CHINA.

~~Prov. No. 594.~~ No. *625*

INDIA FABRICS.

WOOLLENS.

"Kooroon" or "Sulung" cloth. Fine quality.

PRICE IN CASHMERE ABOUT 2*s.* 3*d.* PER YARD.

Length of piece complete 20 yards; width 16½ inches. Weight 3 lbs. 2 ozs.

Made in SULUNG, *between* LASSA *and* CHINA.

~~Prov. No. 592.~~ No. 626

INDIA FABRICS.

WOOLLENS.

"Kooroon" or "Sulung" cloth. Fine quality.

PRICE IN CASHMERE ABOUT 2*s.* 3*d.* PER YARD.

Length of piece 20 yards ; width 17 inches. Weight of entire piece 3 lbs. 2 oz.

Made in SULUNG, *between* LASSA *and* CHINA.

~~Prov. No. 590.~~ No. *627*

INDIA FABRICS.

WOOLLENS.

"Kooroon" or "Sulung" cloth. Fine quality.

PRICE IN CASHMERE ABOUT *2s. 3d.* PER YARD.

Length of piece complete 20 yards; width 16¼ inches. Weight [illegible]

Made in SULUNG, *between* LASSA *and* CHINA.

~~Prov. No. 598.~~ No. 628

INDIA FABRICS.

WOOLLENS.

"Cummerbund" or "Ezarbund;" waist band.

DEEP ENDS GENERALLY.

Length 6 yards 12 inches; width 30 inches. Weight 1 lb. 13 oz.

From HYDERABAD; SCINDE.

~~Prov. No. [illegible]~~. No. 629

INDIA FABRICS.

WOOLLENS.

"Cummerbund" or "Ezarbund;" waist band of a Beloochee male.

NARROW AND COARSE.

Length 5 yards; width 10 inches. Weight 1 lb. 7½ oz.

From BELOOCHISTAN.

~~Prov. No. 599.~~ No. 630

INDIA FABRICS.

WOOLLENS.

"Cummerbund," or waist band.

COARSE BUT STRONG IN TEXTURE.

Length 6 yards 33 inches ; width 12 inches. Weight 1 lb. 7 oz.

From NEPAL.

~~Prov. No. 240.~~ No. *631*

INDIA FABRICS.

WOOLLENS.

"Cumblee" or blanket.

SEWN TOGETHER IN CENTRE TO FORM ONE.

Length 7 yards 18 inches; width 1 yard 22 inches. Weight 7 lbs. Price 18s. 6d.

Made at Dharwar. *Sent from* MADRAS.

~~Prov. No. 882.~~ No. *632*

INDIA FABRICS.

WOOLLENS.

"Cummerbund," or waist band.

Length 5 yards 18 inches; width 9¼ inches. Weight 1lb.

From THIBET.

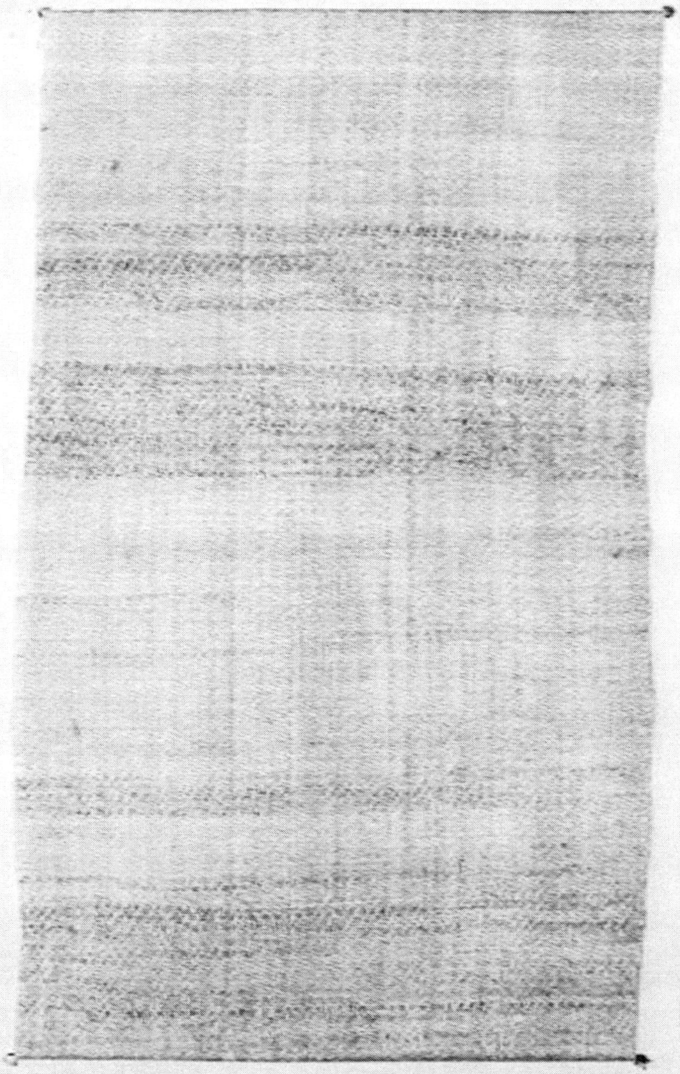

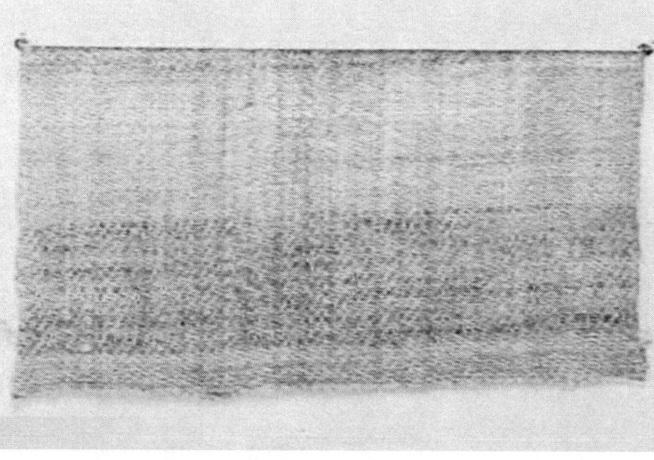

~~Prov. No. 604.~~ No. 633

INDIA FABRICS.

WOOLLENS.

Blanket worn as a scarf by men.

FAIR QUALITY; INDIFFERENT COLOR.

Length 3 yards 3 inches; width 12 inches. Weight 2 lbs. 9 oz.

From DARJEELING.

~~Prov. No. 614.~~ No. 634

INDIA FABRICS.

WOOLLENS.

For men's trowserings.

SUFFICIENT MATERIAL FOR TROWSERS ABOUT 2*s.* 6*d.*

From KANGRA; PUNJAB.

~~Prov. No. 608.~~ No. 635

INDIA FABRICS.

WOOLLENS.

Coarse cloth for clothing.

Length 5 yards 18 inches ; width 15 inches. Weight 2 lbs. 2 oz.

From KANGRA ; PUNJAB.

~~Prov. No. 605.~~

No. 636

INDIA FABRICS.

WOOLLENS.

"Kulloo," blanket.

Length 3 yards 13 inches; width 28 inches. Weight 4 lbs.

Made at KOOLOO. *Obtained from* KANGRA; PUNJAB.

~~Prov. No. 287.~~ No. 637

INDIA FABRICS.

WOOLLENS.

"Cumblee"; blanket or surge cloth; bordered.

TWO SEWN TOGETHER IN CENTRE FORM ONE.

Length 3 yards; width 1 yard 14 inches. Weight 2 lbs. 4 oz. Price 3s.

Made at BANGALORE. *From* MADRAS.

~~Prov. No. 597.~~ No. 638

INDIA FABRICS.

WOOLLENS.

"Kumblee," or blanket. Strong coarse material.

Length 7 yards; width 2 yards 3 inches. Weight 7 lbs. 15 oz. Price 11s. 3d.

From SATTARA; MAHRATTA COUNTRY.

~~Prov. No. 602.~~

No. 639

INDIA FABRICS.

WOOLLENS.

MATERIAL USED PRINCIPALLY FOR MAKING SHAWLS FOR THE "LAMAS."

Length 14 yards; width 9 inches. Weight 2 lbs.

Made at THIBET. *From* DARJEELING.

~~Prov. No. 578.~~ No. 640

INDIA FABRICS.

WOOLLENS.

"Cumblee," or blanket.

Length 5 yards 5 inches; width 1 yard 29 inches. Weight 5 lbs. 9 oz. Price 18s.

From DELHI.

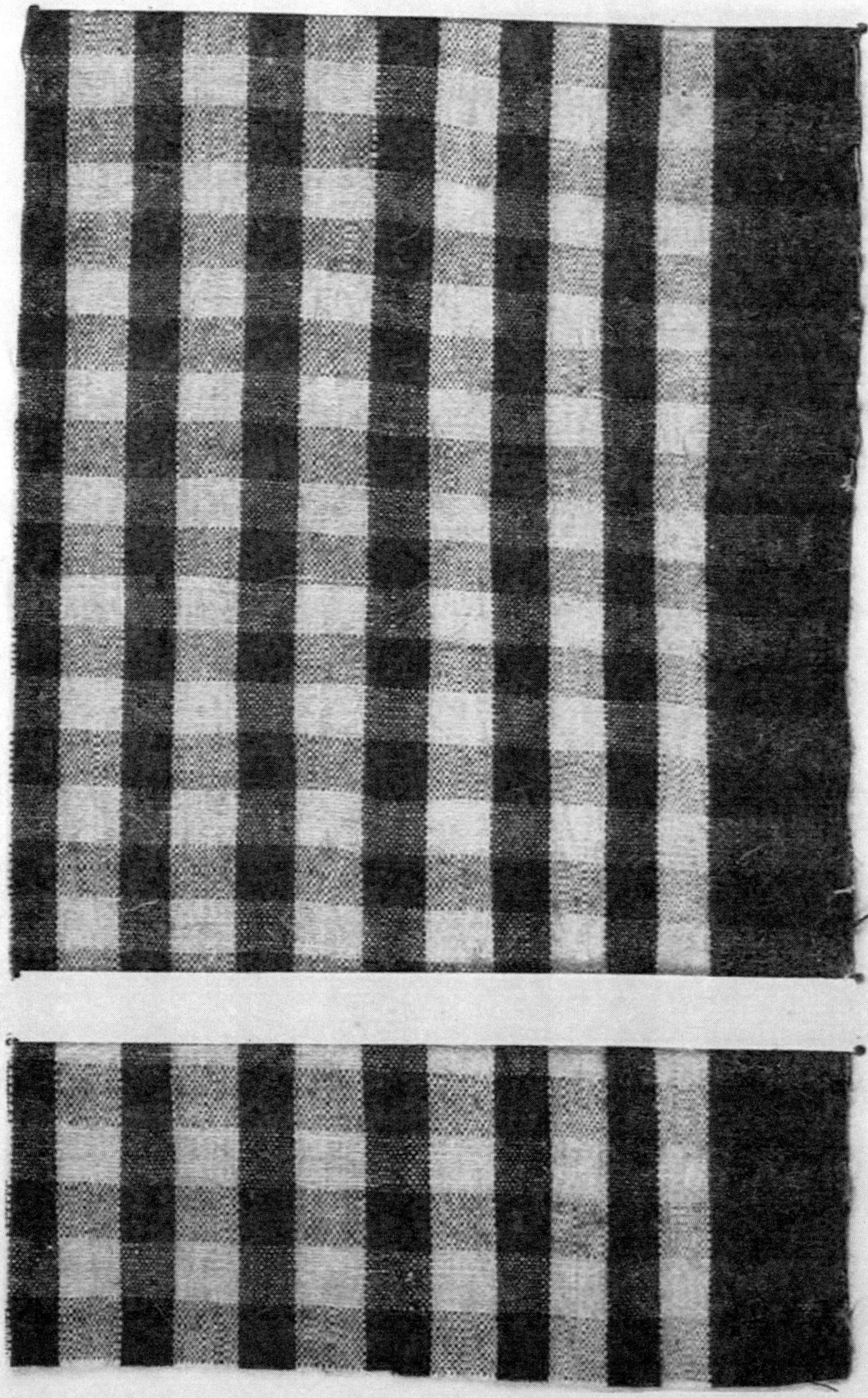

~~Prov. No. 572.~~ No. 641

INDIA FABRICS.

WOOLLENS.

"Cumblee," or blanket. Coarse but strong; the ends fringed.

Length 3 yards 14 inches; width 1 yard 13 inches. Weight 2 lbs. 15 oz. Price 6s.

Made at BEEJAPOOR. *Obtained from* SATTARA.

~~Prov. No. 609.~~

No. 642

INDIA FABRICS.

WOOLLENS.

"Cumblee," or blanket: coarse.

Length 3 yards 19 inches; width 1 yard 16 inches. Weight 3 lbs. 4 oz. Price 4s. 3d.

Made at BEEJAPOOR. *Obtained from* SATTARA.

~~Prov. No. 632.~~ No. 643

INDIA FABRICS.

WOOLLENS.

"Cumblee," or blanket. Black; fringed ends.

Length 7 yards 22 inches; width 2 yards 6 inches. Weight 8 lbs. 8 oz.

From BECKANEER; NORTH-WESTERN INDIA.

THE TEXTILE MANUFACTURERS OF INDIA

JOHN FORBES WATSON

VOLUME:-17

1866

~~Prov. No. 244~~.

No. 644

INDIA FABRICS.

WOOLLENS.

"Cumblee" or blanket: Colored border; coarse texture.

SEWN TOGETHER IN CENTRE WHEN COMPLETE.

Length 3 yards ; width 1 yard 14 inches. Weight 2 lbs. 5 oz. Price 3s. 7½d.

Made at BANGALORE. *Obtained in* MADRAS.

~~Prov. No. 926.~~

No. 645

INDIA FABRICS.

WOOLLENS.

"Cumblee" or blanket. Coarse; fringed ends.

White thread (as shown in most of the patterns) runs down one edge.

Length 3 yards 6 inches; width 1 yard 8 inches. Weight 3 lbs. 4 oz. Price 10s.

Made in BELLARY. *From* MADRAS.

~~Prov. No. 617.~~ No. 646

INDIA FABRICS.

WOOLLENS.

Material used for making cloaks. Colors good.

From SIKIM. *Obtained from* THIBET.

No. 647

INDIA FABRICS.

WOOLLENS.

Material for cloaks, &c.

WORN BY BOTH SEXES. VERY STRONG; COLORS GOOD.

Length 19 yards; width 9½ inches. Weight 6 lbs. 14 oz.

From THIBET.

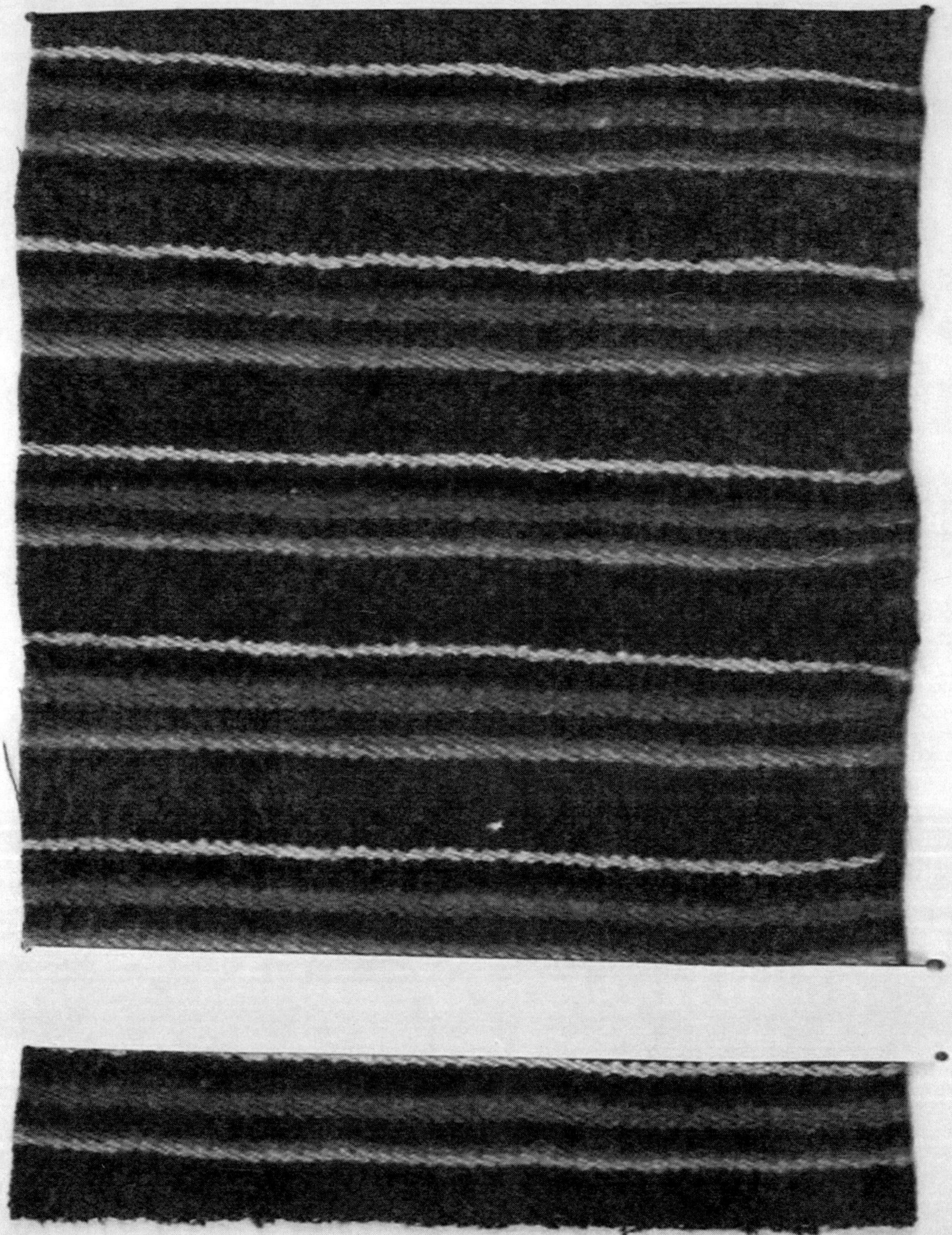

~~Prov. No. 60a.~~ No. 648

INDIA FABRICS.

WOOLLENS.

Material called "Foorook," also "Puttoo."

SUPERIOR QUALITY.

Length 11 yards; width 15 inches. Weight 9 lbs. 11 oz. Price 12s.

From LASSA *in* THIBET. *Obtained in* KANGRA; PUNJAB.

Prov. No. 676.

No. 649

INDIA FABRICS.

WOOLLENS.

Material called "Puttoo."

Length 6 yards 29 inches; width 12 inches. Weight 3 lbs. 7 oz. Price 18s.

From LASSA *in* THIBET. *Obtained at* KANGRA; PUNJAB.

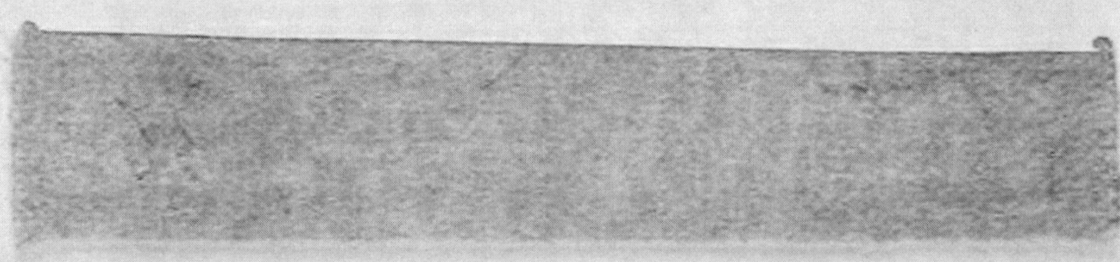

~~Prov. No. 616.~~ No. 650

INDIA FABRICS.

WOOLLENS.

Material used for making coats and cloaks. Very coarse.

USED BY PEASANTS OF KOHAT.

From KOHAT; TRANS-INDUS.

~~Prov. No. 600.~~ No. 651

INDIA FABRICS.

WOOLLENS.

Coarse material.

Length 7 yards 18 inches; width 12 inches. Weight 3 lbs. 8 oz.

From THIBET.

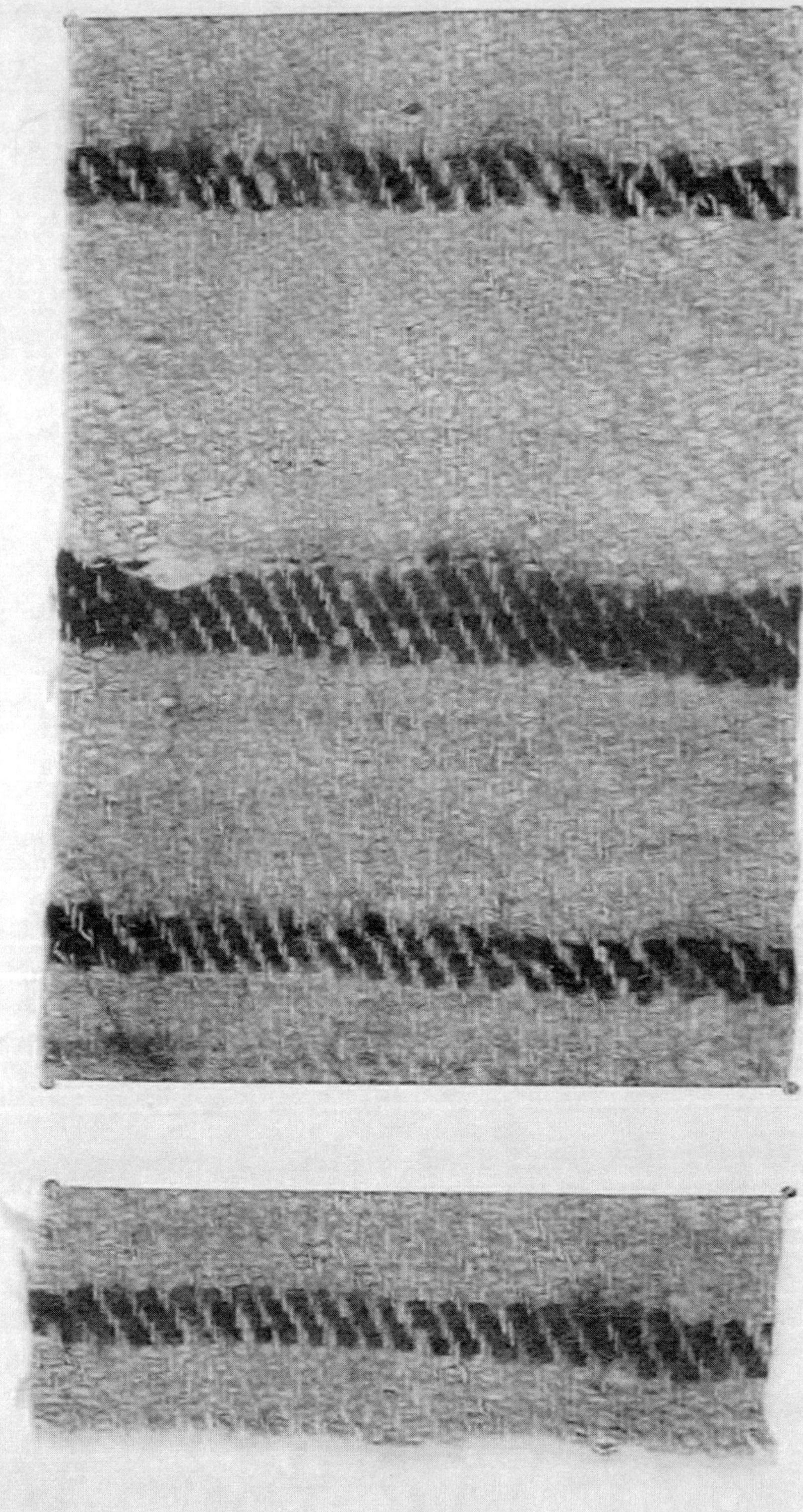

~~Prov. No. 684.~~ No. 652

INDIA FABRICS.

WOOLLENS.

"Loongee," or scarf. Silk borders and ends.

Used for body-clothing during the cold weather, also for bed-covers and saddle-cloths. Sewn together in centre to form one.

Length 5 yards 12 inches ; width 25 inches. Weighs 3 lbs. 14 oz. Price about 4s.

From HYDERABAD; SIND.

~~Prov. No. 598.~~ No. 653

INDIA FABRICS.

WOOLLENS.

Blanket material.

Length 7 yards 9 inches; width 14 inches. Weight 5 lbs. 10 oz.

From THIBET.

~~Prov. No. 238.~~ No. 654

INDIA FABRICS.

WOOLLENS.

"Cumblee" or blanket.

FRINGED ENDS. COARSE QUALITY.

Length 2 yards 27 inches; width 1 yard 2 inches. Weight 2 lbs. 10 oz. Price 1s.

From BANGALORE. *Obtained in* MADRAS.

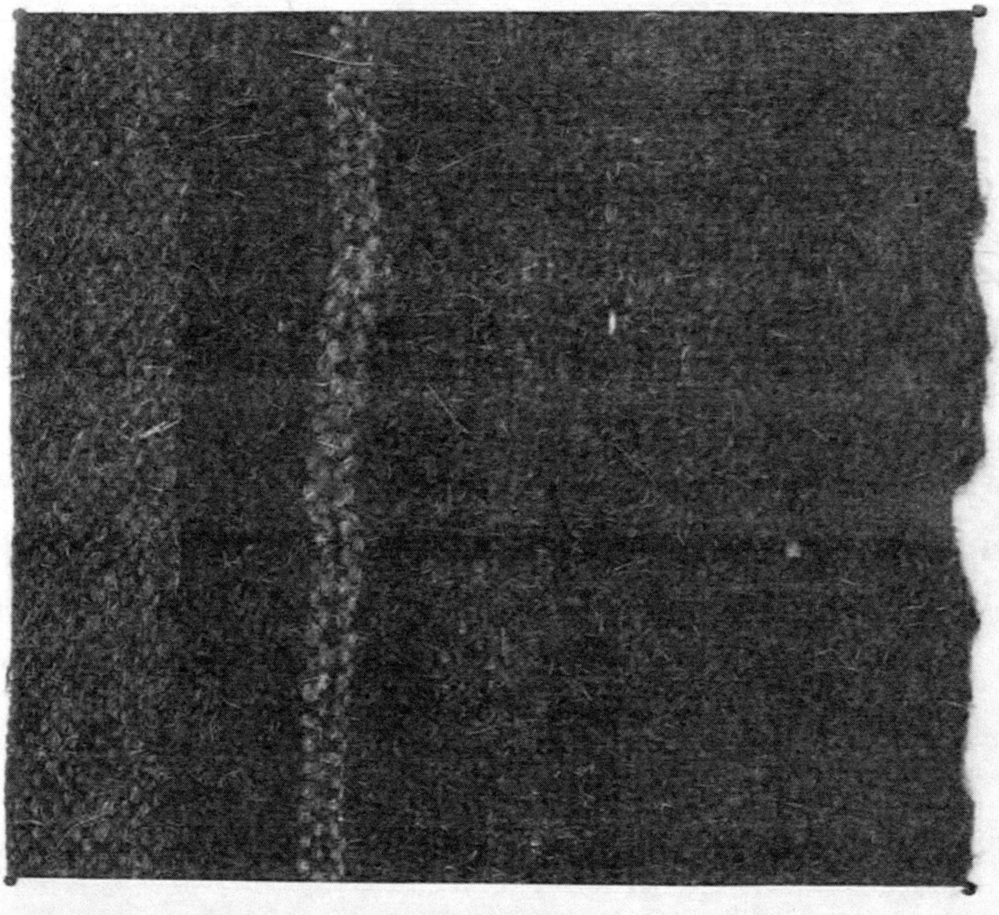

~~Prov. No. 209.~~ No. 655

INDIA FABRICS.

WOOLLENS.

"Cumblee" or blanket.

Mixed with camel-hair. Fringed ends. Coarse quality. Sewn together in centre when complete.

Length of whole 2 yards 20 inches; width 1 yard 18 inches. Weight 5 lbs. Price 1s. 6d.

From BANGALORE. *Obtained in* MADRAS.

~~Prov. No. 571.~~ No. 656

INDIA FABRICS.

WOOLLENS.

"Cumblee" or blanket; coarse quality.

Made and used by the Hill Tribes. Sewn together to form any desired width.

Length of piece 2 yards 9 inches; width 15 inches. Weight 2 lbs.

From KATHMANDOO; NEPAUL.

~~Prov. No. 596.~~ No. 657

INDIA FABRICS.

COARSE WOOL AND HORSEHAIR.
Stuff used for rugs, &c.

Length 18 yards 14 inches; width 10 inches. Weight 10 lbs. 13 oz.

From KANGRA; PUNJAB.

~~Prov. No. 570.~~ No. 658

INDIA FABRICS.

WOOLLENS.

Blanket material.

Length 2 yards 25 inches ; width 1 yard 26 inches. Weight 3 lbs.

From ODYPORE ; RAJPOOTANA STATES.

~~Prov. No. [illegible]~~ No. 659

INDIA FABRICS.

WOOLLENS.

Horse cloth. English pattern.

Length 4 yards; width 2 yards 21 inches. Weight 15 lbs. 15 oz. Price 1l.

From DELHI.

~~Prov. No. 381.~~ No. 660

INDIA FABRICS.

WOOLLENS.

Felt material; colored ends.

USED FOR LEGGINGS, &c.

Length 31 inches; width 18 inches. Weight 9 oz. Price 1s.

From LADAK.

~~Prov. No. 610.~~

No. 661

INDIA FABRICS.

WOOLLENS.

Felted blanket or cloak, to cover the head and body.

Length 1 yard 21 inches; width 2 yards 21 inches. Weight 3 lbs. 12 oz.

From JYEPORE; RAJPOOTANA STATES.

~~Prov. No. 610.~~ No. 662

INDIA FABRICS.

WOOLLENS.

Rough felt-blanket.

Length 3 yards ; width 1 yard 20 inches. Weight $4\frac{1}{2}$ lbs.

From JYEPORE ; RAJPOOTANA STATES.

~~Prov. No. 612.~~ No. 663

INDIA FABRICS.

WOOLLENS.

Blanket material; coarse quality.

Length 3 yards 16 inches; width 2 yards 9 inches. Weight 9 lbs. 14 oz.

From JYEPORE; RAJPOOTANA STATES.

THE TEXTILE MANUFACTURERS OF INDIA

JOHN FORBES WATSON

VOLUME:- 18

1866

~~Prov. No. 633.~~ No. 664

INDIA FABRICS.

CASHMERE SHAWLS.

"Jamewar" (striped shawl). Figured; fine quality.

WORN BY BOTH SEXES.

Length 3 yards 14 inches; width 1 yard 19 inches. Weight 2 lbs. 8 oz. Price 7l.

From KANGRA; PUNJAB.

~~Prov. No. 681.~~ No. 665

INDIA FABRICS.

CASHMERE SHAWLS.

Figured shawl; pine pattern throughout.

Length 3 yards 9 inches; width 1 yard 15 inches. Weight 2 lbs. 2 oz.

From CASHMERE.

~~Piece No. 600.~~ No. 666

INDIA FABRICS.

CASHMERE SHAWLS.

Shawl cloth; pine pattern.

Length 3 yards; width 1 yard 6 inches. Weight 2 lbs. 7 oz.

From CASHMERE.

~~Prov. No. 627~~. No. 667

INDIA FABRICS.

CASHMERE SHAWL CLOTH.

Plain material. Very fine. Good color.

WORN BY BOTH SEXES.

Length 7 yards; width 1 yard 10 inches. Weight 2 lbs. 4 oz. Price 3*l.*

From LOODIANA; PUNJAB.

~~Prov. No. 623.~~ No. 668

INDIA FABRICS.

CASHMERE SHAWL CLOTH.

Plain, 1st quality. Chiefly used for "Chogas."

Length 4 yards 10 inches; width 19 inches. Weight 12 oz.

From CASHMERE.

~~Prov. No. 626.~~ No. 669

INDIA FABRICS.

CASHMERE SHAWL CLOTH.

Shawl cloth, plain. Very fine.

Length 7 yards; width 1 yard 19 inches. Weight 2 lbs. 12 oz. Price 4*l.*

From LOODIANA; PUNJAB.

~~Prov. No. 625.~~ No. 670

INDIA FABRICS.

CASHMERE SHAWL CLOTH.

Shawl cloth, 1st quality. Worn by both sexes.

Length 5 yards; width 28 inches. Weight 1 lb. 1½ oz. Price 2*l*. 15*s*.

From CASHMERE.

~~Prov. No. 624.~~ No. 671

INDIA FABRICS.

CASHMERE SHAWL CLOTH.

Shawl cloth, 2nd quality. Worn by both sexes.

Length 5 yards; width 26 inches. Weight 1 lb.

From CASHMERE.

~~Prov. No. 622.~~

No. 672

INDIA FABRICS.

CASHMERE SHAWL CLOTH.

2d quality.

Length 5 yards 8 inches; width 26 inches. Weight 14½ oz. Price 3*l.*

From CASHMERE.

~~Prov. No. 620.~~ No. 673

INDIA FABRICS.

CASHMERE SHAWL CLOTH.

Shawl cloth, plain. Fine texture.

Length 6 yards 20 inches ; width 1 yard 6 inches. Weight 15 oz. Price 3*l.* 10*s.*

From CASHMERE.

~~Prov. No. 694.~~ No. 674

INDIA FABRICS.

CASHMERE SHAWL CLOTH.

Fine texture.

Length 5 yards; width 26 inches. Weight 14 oz.

From CASHMERE.

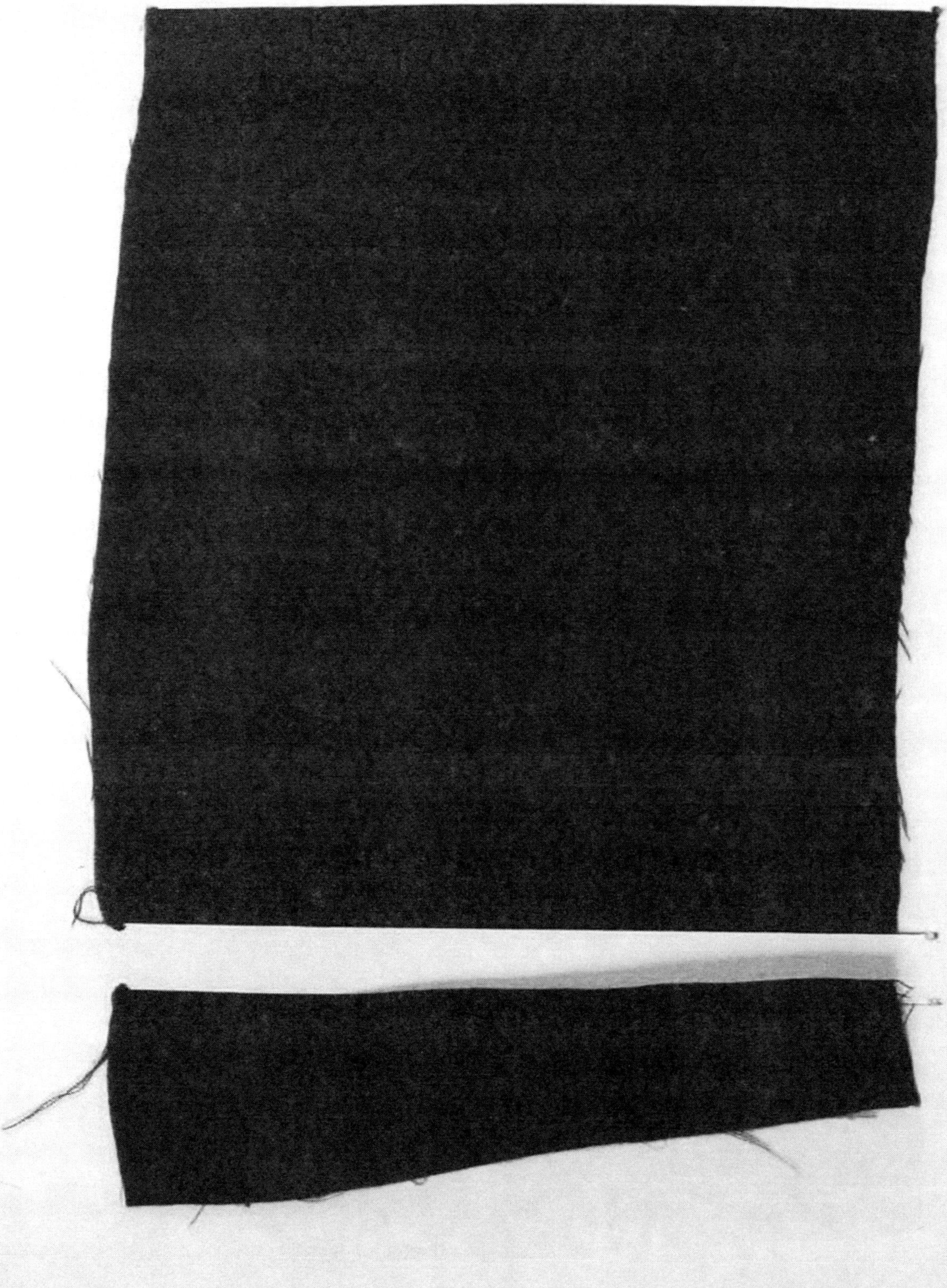

~~Prov. No. 619.~~ No. 675

INDIA FABRICS.

CASHMERE SHAWL CLOTH.

Shawl cloth, 2d quality. Fine color.

Length 5 yards 10 inches; width 25 inches. Weight 15 oz.

From CASHMERE.

~~Prov. No. 629.~~ No. 676

INDIA FABRICS.

CASHMERE SHAWLS.

"Dooputtah" or scarf, (incomplete).

WITH BORDERS (SILVER AND SILK) SEWN ON.

From CASHMERE.

~~Prov. No. 628~~ No. 677

INDIA FABRICS.

CASHMERE SHAWL MATERIAL.

"Loongee" or scarf. With border sewn on.

Length 5 yards 9 inches ; width 1 yard 34 inches. Weight 2 lbs. Price 5*l.* 4*s.*

From CASHMERE.

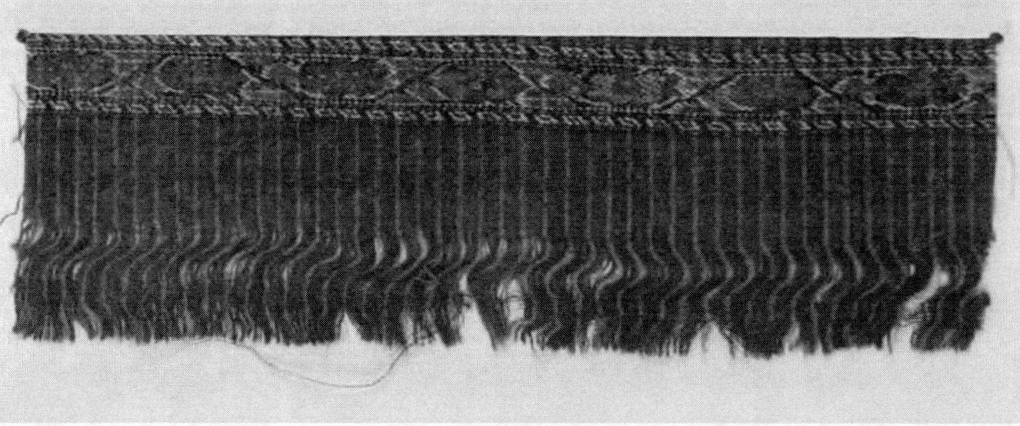

~~Prov. No. 679.~~ No. 678

INDIA FABRICS.

WOOLLEN.

Coarse shawl cloth.

Length 6 yards 21 inches ; width 27 inches. Weight 1 lb. 7 oz.

From LAHORE.

~~Prov. No. 610.~~ No. 679

INDIA FABRICS.

WOOLLENS.

For "Chogas."

WORN BY THE HIGHER CLASSES OF NORTHERN INDIA.

When formed into a cloak costs 2*l.*

From CABOOL.

~~Prov. No. 604.~~ No. 680

INDIA FABRICS.

KID-CLOTH.

"Puttoo," a wrapper. Fine quality.

Woven in half width of 31½ inches; two pieces sewn together in centre forms one complete.

Length 4 yards 29 inches; width 1 yard 27 inches. Weight 4 lbs. 1 oz. Price 3*l*. 4*s*.

From LAHORE.

~~Prov. No. 571.~~ No. 681

INDIA FABRICS.

KID-CLOTH.

"Puttoo." Fine quality.

Length 3 yards 24 inches; width 1 yard 10 inches. Weight 2 lbs. 9 oz. Price 1*l*. 3*s*. 3*d*.

From LAHORE.

~~Vol. No. 607.~~ No. 682

INDIA FABRICS.

KID-CLOTH.

"Puttoo" or wrapper.

Length 9 yards 22 inches ; width 27 inches. Weight 3 lbs. 15 oz.

From THIBET.

No. 683

INDIA FABRICS.

KID-CLOTH.

"Toosee" or Tose cloth.

Length 12 yards 27 inches; width 13 inches. Weight 2 lbs. 15 oz. Price 3*l.*

From BALTISTAN. *Obtained at* KANGRA.

~~Prov. No. 666.~~ No. 684

INDIA FABRICS.

WOOLLENS.

Used as a wrapper.

SEWN TOGETHER IN CENTRE, MAKING AN ENTIRE GARMENT WHEN FINISHED.

Length 2 yards 18 inches; width 1 yard 20 inches. Weight 1 lb. 12 oz.

From LAHORE.

~~Prov. No. 619.~~ No. 685

INDIA FABRICS.

CAMEL HAIR CLOTH. "BURRUCH."

For "Chogas," loose coats like a dressing gown.

From HYDERABAD; SCINDE.

~~Prov. No. 606.~~ No. 686

INDIA FABRICS.

CAMEL HAIR CLOTH, "BURRUCH."

Much worn by Europeans as well as Natives.

Length 8 yards 13 inches; width 13 inches. Weight 1 lb. 14 oz. Price 9s.

From MESHID.

~~Prov. No. 678.~~ No. 687

INDIA FABRICS.

WOOLLENS.

"Dhoosa" or wrapper; silk borders.

Length 3 yards 6 inches; width 1 yard 9 inches. Weight 1 lb. 2 oz. Price 1*l.* 14*s.*

From LAHORE.

~~Prov. No. 687.~~ No. 688

INDIA FABRICS.

WOOLLENS.

"Dhoosa," a scarf with silk borders.

WOVEN IN TWO LENGTHS WITH FAG BETWEEN.

Single one, Length 3 yards 4 inches; width 1 yard 17 inches. Weight 1 lb. 12¼ oz. Price 1*l.* 14*s.*

From LAHORE.

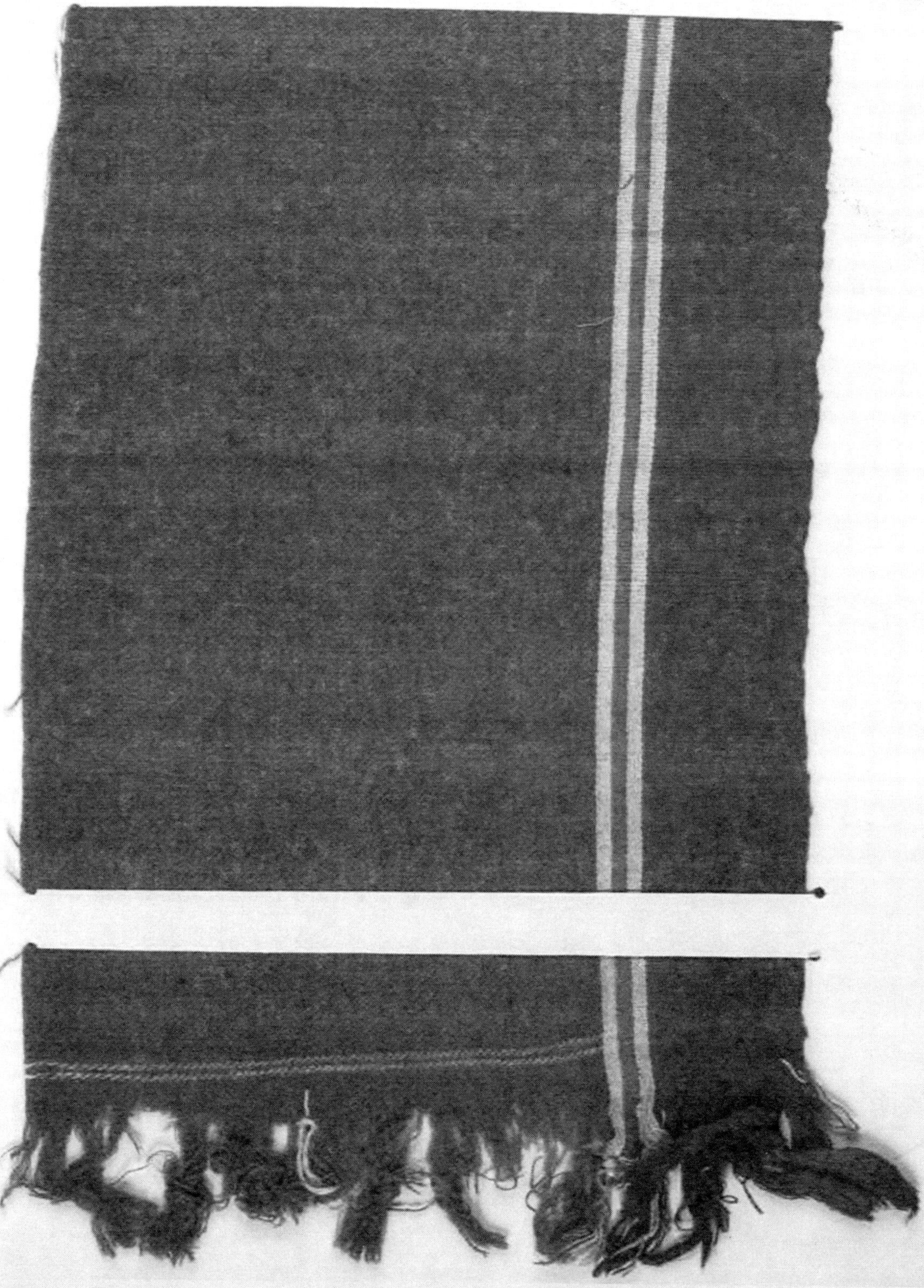

~~Prov. No. [illegible].~~ No. 680

INDIA FABRICS.

WOOLLENS.

"Dhoosa" or scarf, silk borders.

WOVEN IN TWO LENGTHS WITH FAG BETWEEN.

Single one, length 2 yards 14 inches ; width 1 yard 9 inches. Weight 1 lb. 1½ oz. Price 1*l.* 6*s.*

From LAHORE.

~~Prov. No. 377.~~

No. 690

INDIA FABRICS.

WOOLLENS.

"Dhoosa" or scarf; silk borders.

Length 2 yards 30 inches; width 1 yard 6 inches. Weight $14\frac{1}{2}$ oz. Price 1*l*. 6*s*.

From LAHORE.

~~Prov. No. 600.~~ No. 694

INDIA FABRICS.

WOOLLENS.

"Dhoosa" or scarf; silk borders.

Length 3 yards 5 inches; width 1 yard 12 inches. Weight 1 lb. 5½ oz. Price 1l. 15s.

From LAHORE.

~~Prov. No. 576.~~ No. 592

INDIA FABRICS.

WOOLLENS.

Used as a wrap. Inferior quality.

TWO PIECES SEWN TOGETHER FORM ONE.

Length 4 yards 18 inches; width 2 yards 12 inches. Weight 3 lbs. 7½ oz. Price 1*l.* 6*s.*

From LAHORE.

~~Prov. No. 600.~~ No. 693

INDIA FABRICS.

WOOLLENS.

"Loee" or wrap. Good quality.

Length 6 yards 28 inches; width 1 yard 23 inches. Weight 4 lbs. 6 oz.

From BIKANEER; N.W. INDIA.

INDIAN FABRICS.

CARPETS.

No. 695.	No. 696.	No. 697.
Wool. Deep pile.	**Wool. Short pile.**	**Wool. Short close pile.**
From ELLORE.	*From* WURRUNGUL, DECCAN.	*From* BOKHARA.

INDIAN FABRICS.

CARPETS.

No. 698.	No. 699.	No. 700.
Cotton.	**Cotton.**	**Silk.**
Short pile.	**"Suttringee."**	**Short pile.**
From WURRUNGUL, DECCAN.	*From* AGRA.	*From* WURRUNGUL, DECCAN.

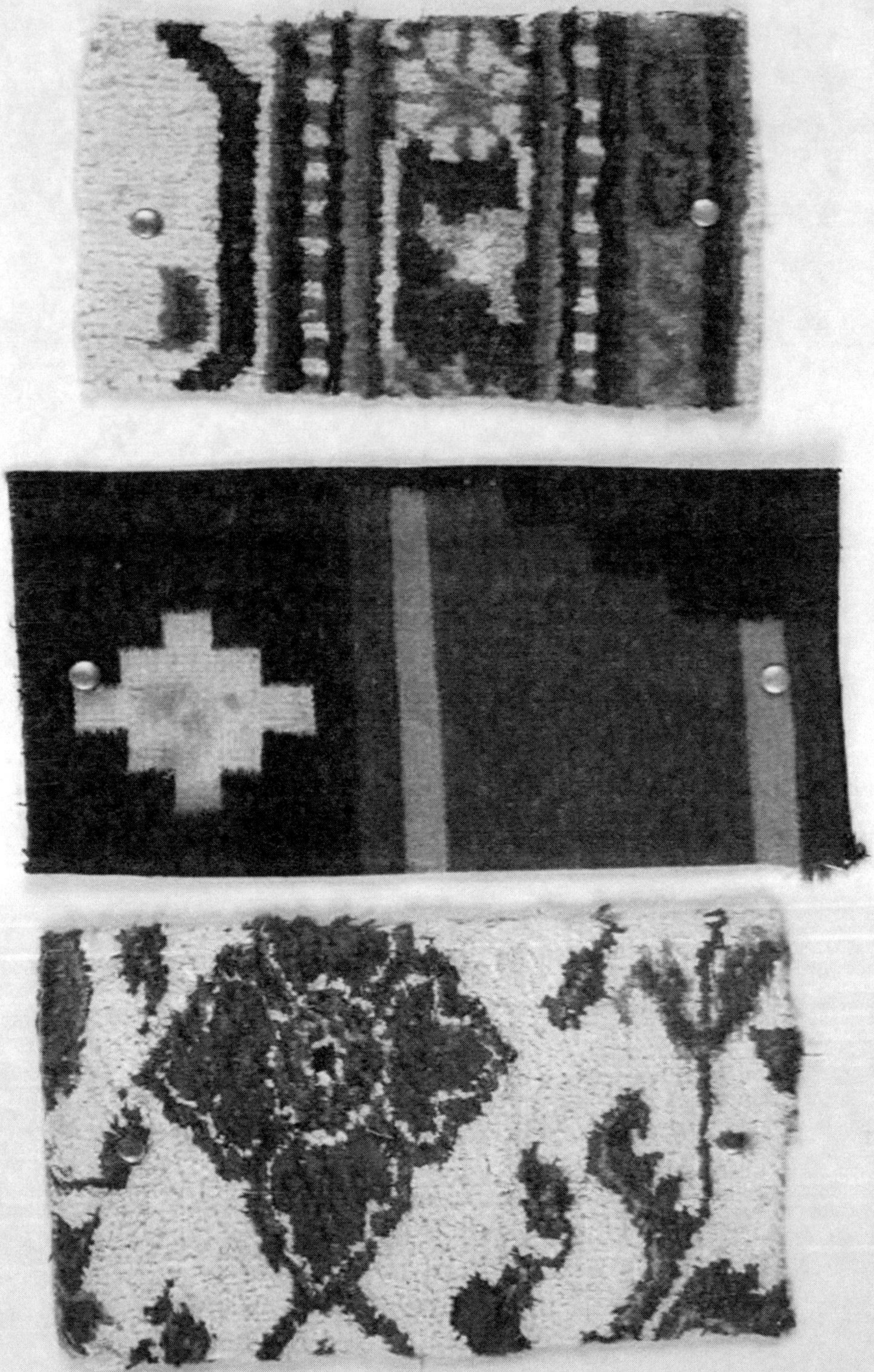